A REAL GOOD WOMAN

SHEBA THE MISSISSIPPI QUEEN

SHEBA

ISBN 13: 978-0-692-97901-3
ISBN 10: 0-692-97901-8

Editing and book design by Carolyn Blakeslee
www.BigCatPress.com

Cover design by Monique Grimme
www.BongoBoyRecords.com

Cover photo copyright ©2014 Paul Carter III, PC3 Photography
www.flickr.com/gp/paul_a_carter/8u8fDq

Printed in the United States of America

In this book some of the names have been changed. "The names have been changed to protect the innocent." If you read this book and think something in it might be about you, then you just might not be so damn innocent! HaHa!
—Sheba

Dedicated
to my Mom, "Madea"

My Story

From Unity's Daily Word, Sunday, July 30, 2017

I am divinely inspired to create and live a full, abundant life.

I am the author of my story. No matter what happens, I choose the meaning I give to events in my life. I see myself through divine perception: as a spiritual victor, an overcomer, and not as a victim of life's circumstances. Inspired by Spirit, I discover deeper understanding and new gifts in myself as I move through challenges.

No part of my story limits the adventure of this day. There are no mistakes or wounds of the past that keep me from living fully now.

I forgive myself and others the errors that occur when we fall short of being our best selves. We are all doing the best we can in this moment. I am free to love, to laugh, and to fully live the abundant life I am divinely inspired to create.

**I came that they may have life,
and have it abundantly.
—John 10:10**

Table of Contents

The beginning

I am sitting here thinking about writing my life story. I guess I should start where it started. I was born in 1953 in Sunflower, Mississippi.

From some of the stories my Mom told me, as a child I had to fight to get attention from people. When I was coming up, they still had a thing about the lighter you were, the better you were treated. I was dark with nappy hair. My twin sister is light-skinned and has what we call very good hair, which means you can get a comb through it.

Looking back on my life and thinking about what I went through, getting love was very hard for me. I love my twin sister and always will, but because of our skin and hair differences, Mom would take us out and people would always play with my sister and not me. She had to tell them, if you cannot play with both of my kids, do not play with either of them. Yet, to me, she seemed to be more for my sister than me—she kind of made me responsible for her. It seemed like my sister couldn't do any wrong and I got blamed for everything.

This went on within my whole family. Kids were being picked over, just because they were dark.

I have a first cousin who is darker than anyone else in the family. Her mom acted like she hated her. Most of her kids were light, but this one was darker; she was treated like an outsider just because she was dark. I always thought that she was beautiful— she had nice smooth skin and pretty white teeth. Even when I went back to Mississippi years later when we were all grown up, she still was like an outsider to the family. The scars that were placed on her as a child have stayed with her.

I remember another lady who had a baby by the boss man. This kid was almost white, but he had that one drop of black blood in him. She worshipped that child—he did not work in the fields, he stayed at home, and she treated her other kids like dogs, even calling them dogs. This is a very bad thing to do to a child, to make them feel they are no good just because of the color of their skin.

My sister would do things and put them on me. She knew they would believe her and not me. She knew she had that kind of control over people, and she used it. One time, she cut a curtain in my grandmother's living room. She told them I did it, and everyone believed her, not me. I knew I was going to get a beating, and I was terrified of whippings.

I remember one time we were playing baseball in the yard. We had a stick of stove wood for a bat. Somehow, the stick came out of my hand and hit my brother. He was bleeding badly. I did not mean to hit him, but everyone thought I did. Every grownup in the house that day beat me—there had to be four or five grownups there that day.

Another time, when I was around eight, my sister and I and some of the other kids were out in the field playing grownup games. I went and told. They said I was lying—and of course, what came of this was a beating.

At this point I had become so afraid of beatings that I started blanking out—I would just sit and stare into space. I wouldn't talk.

And that's when they said I was crazy. They did all kinds of things to bring me out of it. One good thing about it was, I did get some attention. I started thinking to myself, this might work—I could do this for the rest of my life and get the attention I wanted from the people around me.

That all came to an end when my mother took me to a doctor in Jackson. She told Mom that nothing was wrong with me, just don't pay me any attention. How was I to tell them how much I was hurting inside? I was just a child.

Every time I would go into one of my little spells, they would just totally ignore me. Finally I came out of that, but everyone kept it in their heart that I caused the family such grief. I do believe that was another reason my Mom kind of picked my sister over me, because of the way I would act.

Most of my life I have been trying to make people like me any way I could. I remember being treated like something was wrong with me and I tried so hard to fix myself and could not.

I would go around to people's houses and help them any way I could to make somebody like me.

There was a couple who lived next door to my grandmother and granddad's house who showed me a lot of love. They would give me things—food, candy, toys—and let me sleep in bed with them. I knew the wife was sick all the time; I helped her around the house a lot. I can still smell the sweat from her husband and feel his body over me. Something happened one day, and I did not want the candy, toys, food, and the kind of love they were giving me anymore. I locked it up inside and didn't tell anyone.

Another sad day for me was when I started my period. No one had ever told me anything. I was ashamed and thought I had done something wrong.

Predatory people seem to watch and know just what child they can have their way with. Me? They could see me coming from a mile away because I had a sad look on my face. One of my cousins abused me. We were in my grandparents' bedroom; he was leaning back on the bed and picked me up and put me on this thing he had sticking up. It was very painful and I was bleeding. I can still feel that pain inside of me down in my soul. I thought he was going to show me love, not hurt me. This is another thing I didn't tell anyone because I felt they would not believe me. I hated him and was glad when they finally ran him out of town because of something he had done downtown to some white people.

When I got older, I would go with boys just to get them to like me. They would use me and keep on going. I did not like myself. How was I going to get out of my skin? I used to pretend I was someone else who had pretty hair and white skin, and everyone liked me and wanted to be with me. Then I would wake up and feel like a fool. I hated myself. There was only one thing in my life that kept me going: that was my granddad. He would tell me that the way I act and my kindness to people would take me a long way, and it did—but people sometimes mistake kindness for weakness. How can you run from yourself? Wherever you go, there you are. As a young girl, I tried to escape myself through daydreams and whoever would hold me in their arms. Truthfully, they did not hold me, they just had sex.

I'm writing this in hopes that young girls won't go through what I went through. It is so sad what I went through. My Mom, too—she had her first child at the age of 14. A friend of her father's molested her when he stayed at the house.

Years later, I figured out why she was not compassionate with us; there were never hugs and kisses. At times I went to hug her and she pulled away, and I figured out this was from the molestations. Later on in life, I found out how bad this was in me, too.

The way I was treated as a child stayed with me, always trying to show others that I am worthy of being loved. I felt like a poor outsider. The beatings would be with switches, hangers, or whatever they could get their damn hands on. When I grew up, I asked Mom why we kids were beaten like that. She said black people were taught during slavery to beat their children to keep them in line. She said, when black people would walk down the street with their child and a white person approached, that child had to know to keep their head down and not look up at the white person. This was a hard lesson that had to be taught—that child could be taken from you and killed on the spot, and not a damn thing could be done about it.

At one of my family reunions, I found out why my brother and my sister were treated differently from others in my little

My mother and father

hometown. When my Mom was 18, she had a best friend about the same age. She would go to her friend's house to visit, and that friend had a stepfather who became my father. He was about 15 years older than Mom. So that hot little girl took a woman's husband, and out of that came me, my twin, and a brother.

The thing is, my father swore that we were not his children, and his mother said that we were not her son's children. He never was a daddy for us. He did leave his wife for a minute and moved my Mom in with his mother. My grandmother hated her, so he took Mom back home to her parents in shame.

To this day, she regrets what she did. Mom said that after my father had taken her back to her family, he still tried to get involved with her. She said once he went to put his hands on her, wanting her to come back to him—and she took a poke iron and hit him across his shoulder! For months he couldn't use his arm.

Mom was so angry and upset, she would not let our grandmother see us. Mom said this lady was very mean—among other stories she told, Mom said she would cook for my father, and my grandmother would cook too and tell my Dad to eat what she had made and not eat "that mess" Mom made. Years later, when my grandmother was on her death bed, she asked to see my Mom. She wouldn't go to see her. That's just how evil my Mom said this lady was.

Most of my childhood life, I was told that I didn't have a father. Back home, there were many kids who were told that they didn't have a Dad. Lots of mothers had to make it on their own, and what made it so sad was the more kids they had, the more they had to work in the fields. Most of the men had three to four groups of kids from different women, and they didn't stay to take care of them. They just kept on moving and begetting more kids.

To me, the black man had no respect for his women and kids. He felt they were not his responsibility, and in a way, he was right—the white man made that so. My Mom had to take care of all of us all by herself, and she had other kids who were not by my father. That came from a slave frame of mind, and now that I am grown, I see how messed up our black men were. They were taught and trained to do just what they did and got very good at it. Have they been deprogrammed from that slave frame of mind? No, they have not.

Right in my own family there were men who had more than one family. My granddad was one. He was so bad that he fathered a baby with my grandmother's best friend. This broke her heart. She was never the same after that; she was very much in love with him. Later on in life, I did get to meet that uncle.

One of my uncles had three families. He got so good they started naming the kids the same name. Once when I went to Mississippi to visit, my aunt and I were shopping, when she saw a group of people and said they were my kinfolk. She said something that was great of her—she said you cannot take it out on the kids.

My father disowned us, said we were not his kids. My father had about four sets of children, and we all seemed not to like each other. Years later, I was trying to bring our family together, but I was told by one set that they didn't know us and they didn't want to get to know us. This broke my heart, so I stopped trying to reach out.

Dad didn't do anything for us. I remember wanting to be with my father, but he never did come around. Maybe if he'd been there, fewer bad things would have happened to me. In his last days I had a talk with him, and he did claim me as his child.

When my Mom moved us to Florida, there were new ways of dealing with black people and having children. My right to have children was taken from me by people playing God, a pharmaceutical company that made a product by the name of Dalkon Shield. In Homestead, Florida in the 1960s and 1970s, they put into young black girls IUDs that we called loops, to stop them from getting pregnant—but what it really was doing was sterilizing them. My twin, and other girls I went to school with, didn't have children. I found out about the class action lawsuit when I came back to Florida, but I also found out I was too late; the clinic that had the records had been destroyed by Hurricane Andrew. I cannot say to a child, "You do not have a father," but I can say my master made sure of that.

That was home for me

In Mississippi we were very poor. We lived in shabby little houses and had very little food. One house I remember had just one room and didn't have a floor; it was on the ground. In the winter, for heat, we would make a fire in the middle of the floor. In the summertime the ground was cool, so we had natural air conditioning for those hot Delta summers.

We lived in one house that was a little bigger, but we only lived in half of it because the other half had been torn down. This house was built off the ground, but it had a big hole in the floor. You could look through that hole and see snakes and frogs. I guess that is why I have such fear of snakes and frogs to this day.

Later we moved into a "shotgun house," so called because they were long and narrow; you could take a shotgun and shoot

A row of shotgun houses

straight through it. There were rows of them along the Mississippi River. These houses had three to four rooms, and a family of nine or ten, sometimes more, lived in them.

Food was something we never had enough of. I remember many nights going to bed hungry. Mom would give us what she had in the house. Sometimes that would be bread and water with sugar in it. There were times when we did have food—the state had big trucks that would bring supply food out to the poor. They would give us flour, cheese, sugar, beans, and peanut butter. This, I do believe, was done once a year. For the rest of the year, we had to do what we could to survive. We would dig worms to go fishing; sometimes, when we would find a small lake or a little pond, we would jump into the water and muddy it up, and the fish would just come to the top. All we had to do was pick them up—this was called "mudding."

Black molasses and biscuits, and salmon balls, were a big thing for us. My Mom knew how to stretch that can of fish by putting cornmeal, flour, and onions in it. Normally a can of fish would make about ten salmon croquettes, but my mom could get 20 to 25 out of one can.

Beans were big, too—she would put in a piece of fatback, and the race was on—the first to find the fatback got the prize.

When we would get to the fields with our lunch, whatever we could find to put food on became our plate. Most of the time it was a leaf or a piece of paper, whatever could hold those molasses biscuits. We used our fingers; at that time there was no such thing as a knife and fork. Utensils were something I found out about many years later when we moved to Florida.

There were times when there was plenty of food, such as at hog-killing time, when

Mississippi cotton fields

14

people would take their hogs to the slaughterhouse. The white people gave to the poor all the parts of the pig they didn't want. We would get the feet, tail, pig ears, hog guts (called chitterlings), and the head. They had something on a hog called Mountain Oysters; the grownups wouldn't tell us children what they were, but later on in life I found out. Redd Foxx used to say, "We'd eat everything on a hog—if we could catch the grunt we would eat that." My mom would take that hog head and make souse, or hog head cheese. She cooked the whole head down real slow all night and next day pick out the bones. She would put it into a loaf pan, put it in the ice house so it could chill, and it was so tender you could cut it with a fork.

There was a lesson we kids taught our Mom: on a farm, do not let the kids make pets out of the food you are going to eat. My Mom was a young mother, and there were a lot of things she just didn't know. Someone had given her some chickens so we could have eggs. We made a friend out of one rooster; we named him Willie. During one of those hard times, way before slaughtering time when the food was very low, when there were about eight of us, we found out that our sweet Mom had killed and cooked Willie so we could have food on the table. All of us looked at her like she was crazy to do that to our friend. We looked at that woman pick up a piece of that chicken and put it in her mouth, and we all started to cry. I think we all walked around for days hating her for doing that to our friend. I don't know what she finally did with that chicken—we never did eat any of it.

I remember mornings, just before daybreak, getting ready to go to the fields. My sister was a hard one to wake up in the mornings; it would be like bringing her back from the dead. I am sure she didn't want to face the day out in that Mississippi Delta sun. Those Delta summers were hot and steamy. I remember looking at the Mississippi mud all dry and cracked on the ground—if you walked across it, it would burn your feet. I don't know how we made it in those cotton fields, chopping and picking cotton in the hot sun all day long. I remember people having fainting spells, bad nosebleeds, and sun strokes.

There is one thing that kept us going, and that was singing. We would start to sing, and it seemed like everything just went away. The heat from that big yellow sun, the hunger pangs, all of it just went away. This is where the soul of my music came from—those cotton fields of Mississippi. I didn't get it from school books, or from someone teaching me; it came from within. Even when we were not in the fields singing, we were in church or on the porch late evenings singing.

And sometimes at night, that Delta moon would be so big and beautiful you could see everything, and we would work through the night. I can see that white cotton just beaming across the fields, like a blanket of snow. It was truly beautiful to me as a child, and all we did was keep on picking, chopping, and singing.

Then there was the fear. So much fear. A lot of brutalities went on back home. There were times when I would see the fear on grownups' faces.

I remember when my older brother went to be a part of the march with Martin Luther King. I was overcome with fear, and my imagination went completely crazy. Fear was something I had as a child and I never shared it with anyone. I kept it within myself.

At night, my imagination ran wild. In that one-room shack, the only light we could see was the moonlight coming through the window. Here's how one of the stories in my head went. You hear your Mom and Dad. Mom is crying and Dad is scared, saying these people are coming to the house to kill him, and there is no place and no one for him to go to. You hear a lot of noise outside. Then you see lights and hear a voice shout, "Nigger, come out!" Your Mom begs him not to go, then a voice says, "If you don't come out we will burn the house down." Your father looks over at you and your other brothers and sisters. You see the fear in his eyes. He knows he is going to die. Your Dad walks outside in hopes they will make it quick. The only thing is, these people do not want it quick—the slower you die, the better it makes them feel. They come into the house and get you and your brothers and sisters, so this can be a lesson. Then you see them put a rope around him and pull him away. For a very long time you can hear the screams of his voice in your head as you see the arms and legs come off his body. When they are finished with your Dad, some of the men come into the house and rape your Mom and your sisters and leave. These are some of the things I would think about. This is the type of fear that I felt.

Singing in my soul: My folks

When I was a child, we would sing in the cotton fields to make the day go by. The work was very hard and singing was a way to keep our mind off how hard it really was. During the wintertime when it was cold, we would just sit around the stove or fireplace and sing.

There were a lot of singers around me. Anytime I felt sad about something, I would go and be by myself and sing to feel better. This is something I picked up from my grandmother; when she was down, she would do a lot of mourning. One place she went was to her backyard by the peach tree, where she would mourn and cry.

I came from a background of singers. On both my Mom's side and my Dad's side, all had great voices.

My Mom and my aunt both had beautiful voices, and when they sang together they sounded like angels. They would go to different churches and compete, and most of the time they won. I remember I was around seven or eight years old when they started making me stand up to sing. They would listen and just cheer me on, and whenever I made a mistake they would help me out. Most of my childhood, all the way up to my teens, I was very shy about getting up to sing in front of people. Most of the time I had to be pushed onto the stage.

From what I was told, my father was a great singer. My Mom said the high notes he could hit were unbelievable. Back in the early '40s to the late '50s, my Daddy had a group called the Happy

Band Boys. This was during the time that B.B. King was on a gospel radio station out of Inverness, Mississippi. My Dad and his group would go there on Sunday and sing on that station. My Dad had three children from my Mom—my brother, myself, and my twin—and the three of us can sing. We never really got to know him or his people, but we did inherit singing from them.

I have always wondered why so many great singers came out of the Delta. I found out that during slavery, all kinds of African slaves from many different tribes were brought here, and many of them had different kinds of talents. Slaves learned all types of trades and crafts such as blacksmithing, shoemaking, and midwifery. What was in the soul was a song they didn't learn, it was a part of them—and that's where America's first music came from, the souls of the slaves.

I found out later on why in the beginning blues players like Jimmie Reed and Robert Johnson were so off of the beat—because the blues had no definite beat. In fact, during slavery, the slaves were not allowed to have drums because then they could communicate with each other. So anything that a slave could beat on was taken away.

I'm going to talk about something that was a result of slavery, and why we African-Americans are not close as a family. I have no idea what part of Africa my ancestors came from. Someone said that most of the slaves brought to America came off the West Coast of Africa. Once slaves were brought into the ports of America, everything and everyone got totally lost, because they were sent all over the place. The slaves that were of the same tribe, and spoke the same language, had to be broken up. If this was not done, they could retaliate and break free.

On my Mom's side, I couldn't find out much about my grandmother and grandfather—when a slave would escape, they would change their name and tell no one where they came from. This is what happened to my grandfather. He was about 12 or 13 years old when he did something wrong where he was born, and he ran away, changed his name, and told no one where he came from.

As a very young boy he worked on the levee in New Orleans, around the turn of the century. That is where he met my grandmother. She was with a man who was very mean to her;

my grandfather got her and ran away with her to Mississippi. My mother said my grandfather had one sister who used to come to Mississippi to visit him; her name was Judy and she was white. I am sure this came from their shared father, who my Mom said was a white man. Back then you were considered black if you had one drop of black blood in you, and I'm sure he had that one drop.

Mom said they used my grandfather's father for what they called a stock Nigger. They would take him around to different plantations to impregnate young girls. He had one very dark African slave woman he was in love with. The only thing he asked of the slave master was to be allowed to take her with him wherever he went.

There is not much I know about my grandmother on my mother's side, only that my great-grandmother's name was Martha. I was named after her. She was a small woman and part Blackfoot Cherokee.

On my father's side, I can go back as far as my slave great-great grandmother who was born in 1844 and passed away at the age of 53. Born in Alabama, her name was Phillis Booker. Most of her life she was a housekeeper, and someone cared enough for her to bury her properly. I was able to find a death certificate and learn where she was buried in Alabama.

One thing I found out was that some of the census-takers in the United States were giving people the wrong names, wrong birthdates, wrong death dates. Phillis Booker, with Frank Booker, had my father's grandfather, Nelson Booker—and Nelson Booker fathered my father's father, who was Herbert Booker. Herbert Booker fathered my Dad, Leroy Booker. I couldn't find any other information on my slave great-great grandfather, Frank Booker. Following the U.S. Census back to 1880, my people were all from the hills of Alabama.

Later, my father's folks moved from Alabama to Rolling Fork, Mississippi. This is where my father was born. He met my mother in Sunflower, which is about 60 miles away. Rolling Fork is where the great blues singer Muddy Waters was born. He just might be part of my family.

Still in Mississippi

My Mom had her first child at age 14; by the time she was 20, she had five children. The only thing she was told by her Mom and other grownups was to keep her dress down. She was molested starting when she was three years old, and she remembers being fondled for most of her young life. The touch and the smell of that person have stayed with her all her life. So when she grew up, she was not able to show compassion to her children, or anyone. When someone would go to hug her, she would pull away.

She should have been told more than just to keep her dress down, and they should have watched the people who were around her. Those guys were so slick-talking that she did not need to pull her dress up—they would just cut her drawers off. My oldest brother was from a man that my grandparents let stay at their house for a few nights. This is one of those people that took advantage of a child. This man got into my 14-year-old Mom's drawers; nine months later, my oldest brother was born. Back then, anytime you got a girl pregnant you were made to marry. My Mom married the man and she hated his guts. They were married for about ten months and then he just disappeared.

Another thing back then—the grandparents would take away the first child. When my brother turned four months old, they took him out of Mom's bed and raised him. He just doesn't know what it would have been like to have been raised by a 14-year-old child.

I was born in 1953 with my twin sister on a plantation in Sunflower County, delivered by a midwife named Miss Mary. For some reason, a doctor had to be there too. After I came, the midwife told the doctor that something else was still in my Mom.

Eight minutes later, here came another child, my sister, Mary. That's when my Mom got pissed off. My Mom was so upset at us that she didn't want to look at us or touch us. She was upset because our father had disowned us and had gone back to his wife. I'm sure she was ashamed how we were conceived by my Dad; today she says she regrets doing that.

By this time, besides my oldest brother Clayborne, who was taken away by my grandparents because Mom was just 14, my Mom already had my brother Joseph, who was four, and my brother Donald, who was two. So at 20 years old, for her we were number four and five, Martha and Mary.

My grandmother never really talked to my Mom about sex. Back in the day, people never talked to their kids about those things. My Mom says she was just having sex because she liked the way it made her feel. So when each baby came along, one of the things she had in mind was whether she was going to keep it. Thank God she did, because that's why I'm here today.

49W We were sharecroppers on a plantation off Highway 49W, on Highway 3, off in the woods, in a place called Morgan City. My Mom would talk to us about being respectful to the boss man and all of his kids. We had to be respectful to all white people, even their dogs. Even when white children were babies, we had to say "Yes, Sir" and "Yes, Ma'am," and we had to hold our heads down. When I was a child I thought white people were angels.

In Sunflower, most of the white people lived across the river. You had to go through town and across the river to get to their neighborhood. The first thing you would see is how well kept the yards were; my granddad was one of the ones who would take care of some of those yards. You would see the beautiful brick houses, and in those houses mostly black maids were keeping them clean and doing all the cooking. The school they had put our school to shame; they had the best of everything.

When you came back across the river through the town back into the black neighborhood, it wasn't so nice. The black people living along the riverbank lived in little huts that I believe used to be slave quarters. They looked like some of those pictures you see on television about Africa, with the baby sleeping, and the flies in and out of their mouth.

One incident that happened made me think of the difference about white people. I found out that Mississippi did have its share of poor white people; they were called poor white trash. We went to move into a house some white people had moved out of. These people had pooped all over the house, and trash was everywhere. They were very nasty. I was shocked because these were white people, and white people weren't supposed to be like that.

While working on the plantation, I remember we had what we called a straw boss and the big boss. You never went to the big boss—everything was done through the straw boss. I remember working in the fields and the straw boss would ride around on his horse making sure we were doing what we were supposed to do.

The straw boss was the one who would weigh the cotton and take it to the gin. Every year, the plantation owner (the big boss) would have the straw boss give their sharecroppers $15 (sometimes $20), a slab of fatback, and a 50-pound bag of pinto beans. This had to last through the winter. Thinking back, those pinto beans sure were good, and to make it even better we sometimes had cornbread.

When my sister and I were four, we were put to work in the fields. They had little cotton sacks made just for kids and a little hoe for chopping cotton. Mom trained us so well that at that age we wouldn't chop down any cotton, just the weeds in the cotton. On this plantation, another family of sharecroppers—a man, his wife, and three kids who were older than we were—had the crop next to ours. We would out-pick them, just my Mom and six of us little kids. My brother was bringing in at the age of 10 close to 300 pounds of cotton a day. My Mom would

Straw boss checking off cotton brought in by pickers, Marcella Plantation, Mileston, Mississippi Delta, 1939. Photo by Marion Post Wolcott for the Farm Security Administration

bring in about the same, maybe a little more. My other brother Donald picked about 200; the rest of us kids did our best. (Lily C. was three years younger than Mary and me, and James was the baby at that time.) That guy just could not understand how my mother did it with six little ones. We were bringing in three bales of cotton a week. This man was bringing in with his family only about two bales a week.

Working in those cotton fields was very hard. That hot Delta sun can be vicious. The only thing that kept us going was the singing. If you didn't know how to take care of yourself, you could die in those cotton fields. I remember being sick and dizzy and my nose bled a lot. Anytime someone got sick, they would take you out of the field and put you under a shade tree to cool off, then put you back to work.

We were working most of the time near Highway 49W, where we would see all kinds of traffic going by—mostly big trucks hauling sugar cane, soybeans, and cotton; and the Greyhound bus.

What I remember most of all is what my grandmother would say every time she saw that old Greyhound bus go by. She would say, "Going my way? but it just ain't my day," and she would be so sad, with tears in her eyes. It seemed like everybody would stop and watch that Greyhound bus go by and disappear in a cloud of dust. As if on cue, everyone paused until the bus was out of sight, and then they would bend their backs and go back to chopping, picking, and singing.

Before moving off the plantation, my Mom got a home in town. Back then, if you saw an old house in the country, you could pay someone to bring it into town. A lady named Miss Norris was selling houses, and she sold one to my granddad—a house he saw in Greenwood—and had them bring it to Sunflower. My Mom found a $350 house somewhere in the country; my granddad bought it for her and she paid him back.

Our shotgun house was placed one door down from our grandparents, and my grandmother didn't like that. There was a church in between the two houses, and it was the same church that we all attended. My grandmother didn't like the idea that we were moving so close to her—in her heart, she was trying to teach my mother a lesson. My Mom had all those babies and she wanted her to take care of them. Grandmother knew that my grandfather had a soft spot in his heart for his only girl; there were four boys, and Mom was the only girl. Plenty of times my grandfather stepped in to help us, and from what my Mom told me, he would tell her not to tell my grandmother.

Back in Mississippi, the women would get together to make quilts. They would take all the old clothes that had holes in them, cut pieces out, and sew them together to make the quilts. They would get cotton and have us kids pick the seeds out. They would place the cotton on top of one layer of cloth and place another layer of cloth on top of the cotton, and sew it up. I've seen some beautiful quilts in my day.

African-American women holding quilts and rugs, 1934, Florida Photographic Collection

My grandmother used to do a lot a canning. She would buy peaches by the bushel, and sometimes apples. She would can this stuff and it would last for years. Sometimes biscuits and canned fruit was all we had to take us through those long, cold winters.

Mississippi had some bitter, cold winters. They said it was so cold, if you threw a pail of water in the air it would freeze before it hit the ground! I remember seeing my grandfather and some of the other men's mustaches or beards frozen while cutting wood or doing whatever else needed to be done outside.

During the winters, most of the time we really didn't do much. We stayed in the house, and we kids made up all kinds of games to play with one another. I used to love to sit by that old potbelly stove and watch the wood burn down to ashes.

In the summertime, there was plenty to do, including things

we could do to make extra money. Going out to pick blackberries to sell was fun. Most of the time we were eating more than we could sell, and we had to be very careful about the snakes—they love eating blackberries, too. My grandmother would make some beautiful blackberry pies and blackberry dumplings.

Another big thing was picking pecans. Back then we called them "puck corn" and we made good money selling pecans.

Another thing we did at the end of cotton-picking time—after everything had been picked for the season, they had what they called "stripping cotton." You went into the field and put everything left in the cotton sacks. I think this was used for the next crop. This paid very little, but it was a lot of fun for us kids.

I didn't see many of the hard times as a child, but I do remember the hunger pangs. I do remember when there wasn't enough food. We kids used to go along Highway 49W and find bottles to sell; we earned a penny a bottle, and some paid a little more.

The Mississippi Delta is a rich and beautiful place. That Mississippi mud is rich with minerals, and it was clear how people there could grow such wonderful crops. During the summertime, you could see fields of giant daisies everywhere—it seemed as if they went on for miles. I have never in my life seen such beautiful sunflowers as I've seen in Sunflower, Mississippi. I guess that's why they named the town Sunflower, because of all the sunflowers that naturally grow there. There were all kinds and all sizes, more than ten to fifteen feet tall and as big as the moon. They grew in all kinds of beautiful colors—brown and gold, green, yellow, pink—not just yellow and brown.

On the way out of Mississippi

My Mom used to daydream about leaving Mississippi as a little girl. She felt good just thinking about it. Her dream as a child was to grow up and become a teacher. When Mom had her first baby at 14, that killed her dream. My Mom became a good field hand and showed the white people she was a hard worker. This is what kept her out of trouble—working hard, and knowing that when she needed anything from the white folks, to go to the back door.

Sunflower, Mississippi was pretty rough. I remember the store where the Greyhound bus would stop to pick up and drop off people. The owner of the store had a talking bird in his store. When a black person came in, this bird would say, "Nigger stealing, Nigger stealing!" whether that black person was stealing anything or not. That bird would not shut up until the owner came over. I always wondered how they trained that bird to know the difference between a black person and a white person. My Mom did not like that man and did not go into his store; he was very nasty to black people.

All kinds of incidents happened when my Mom was a little girl that turned her against the state of Mississippi. Mississippi has very rich soil, and all kinds of fruits and vegetables were grown there. Mom said that one summer she and her brothers went out to pick blueberries for a white lady. They had a two-and-a-half-pound water bucket that they filled with blueberries to sell to her, but when they came back with the blueberries, she didn't want to give them the money. My Mom told her they had worked very hard picking those berries and they wanted their money. The lady went to my Mom's Dad and told him that she was being very sassy with her. Back in those days, you did not talk back to white people like that, no matter what they said or did—you just took it and went on. I'm not sure what happened or what kind of punishment she got, but it was so devastating that it was a major turning point in her life pertaining to Mississippi.

Mom told me that once she was downtown in Sunflower and went into a store. She was looking around and put her hands on a dress. The white man asked her what she wanted, and she told him she was just looking. He told her to get out of the store, and my Mom said she backed out of the store, because she knew if she turned around, that man was going to kick her. She never went back to that store. Those kinds of things really hit my Mom hard and turned her against Mississippi.

My Mom remembers when black people had to be off the streets in Sunflower by a certain time. She said a policeman would go through the street ringing a bell at 11:00 p.m. and everyone had to be gone. If you were caught on the street later than that, you could go to jail. Most people would go home, or to the nearby town of Greenwood, or they would go out in the country to some juke joint and hang out.

It was only on Saturday that black people would walk up and down the street with their kids, just enjoying the afternoon. Mom loved dancing; she would go out on Saturday night to the juke joint to dance and have a few drinks. After dancing all night, she would wake up on Sunday and go to church to sing. People would tell her, you can't do that dancing on Saturday night and come to church on Sunday, you can't serve two Gods. She made the choice to keep on dancing and serve the Lord at home.

On some weekends, my aunt, who was my Mom's brother's wife, would keep us kids while Mom went to town. Other weekends, Mom would keep my aunt's kids while she went to town. They even used to nurse each other's babies. My Mom had ten children, but my aunt outdid her by having thirteen.

Food was scarce. One of the things Mom used to talk about was how poor we were. One of her favorite stories was how one day a rabbit gave his life so we could have some food. Every time she told this story, she was proud. One day when we all were very little—none of us were big enough to go to the fields to work—Mom had very little food, and what she had she gave to us. She was out chopping cotton when around 10:00 a.m. she saw a little rabbit, and she ran and got a big rock and killed it. She was so happy to have some meat for us to eat to go with the flour. My Mom was so happy praising God and thanking God and thanking that little rabbit. Even today, when she talks about that rabbit, she lights up. Thanks to you, little rabbit, wherever you are, for making my Mom happy, and helping me to grow.

In 1963, after the birth of Curtis, my newest brother, his father—they called him Shorty—just walked off and left her, and she never heard anything from him again. He was very mean to Mom and us kids.

She had some mean men in her life. I remember a man by the name of Mr. Otis; he was someone she dated for just a little while. On a Saturday night after leaving the juke joint, my mother and a friend were on their way home when this man followed them home. Mom wanted to break up with him and he didn't want to break up, so he was going to make her stay with him. When they went into the house, he started banging on the door, wanting to get in. He was trying to break the door down and knock out the window. She told him to leave her alone but he would not stop.

She had a shotgun and shot up into the ceiling, but this fool kept on trying to break into the house. She had no choice but to do what she did. Mom put the shotgun on her shoulder and took a moment to think, because she was going to shoot through the door. She and this man were the same height, so if she shot standing, she was sure she would hit him in the heart. So she kneeled down on the floor and shot him through the door.

After that, she heard someone moaning, so she ran out the back door. She had the shotgun in her hand as she ran to the boss man's house to let him know what she had done. He told her to first put down the shotgun. She was sure she had killed the man and that she would be going to jail. However, that man had a bad reputation in town for being lazy and not working. Back then, white people had great respect for black people who worked hard, and my Mom was a hard worker. She didn't go to jail and she never had any more trouble out of that man. He did survive, and if they saw each other when walking down the street, he would cross the street to the other side.

When my Mom got tired of the bad treatment from the plantation bosses and the bad men in her life, she was just about ready to leave the Mississippi Delta. By this time there were eight of us, and my baby brother Curtis was 11 months old and not yet walking. We had worked the whole summer and the boss man gave Mom $12 for all the work we had done, just $12 to make it through the whole winter. She took that money to buy some coal so we could have heat for the winter. We had a deep freezer with meat put up for the winter; she was paying $10 a month on it. The lights were turned off, so we lost all that meat, and then the man came and took his freezer, so we were left with nothing.

At this point she decided she'd had enough. Winter was coming and there would be nothing in Sunflower for us to survive on. Mom made up her mind that she was going to leave and go to South Florida, because there was work down there in the tomato and bean fields.

In the years leading up to when our Mom got us out of Mississippi, the 1960s Civil Rights movement was happening. In fact, as early as 1941, A. (Asa) Philip Randolph had planned a march on Washington to eliminate employment discrimination in the defense industries. However, after President Roosevelt issued Executive Order 8802 and created an agency to oversee the Order, which barred racial discrimination, the march was canceled.

Randolph and Bayard Rustin were the planners of the August 28, 1963 march in Washington.

Civil rights activists became increasingly combative in 1963 to 1964, and Mississippi NAACP Field Director Charles Evers said, at a public NAACP conference in February, 1964, that "non-violence won't work in Mississippi … if a white man shoots at a Negro in Mississippi, we will shoot back." In Jacksonville, Florida, a riot happened—black youths threw Molotov cocktails at police. In April 1964, Malcolm X gave his famous "The Ballot or the Bullet" speech. Also in the spring of 1964, four prominent Massachusetts women, including 72-year-old Mrs. Mary Parkman Peabody, the mother of the governor of Massachusetts, made headlines for attempting to dine at a St. Augustine motel in an integrated group; her arrest made national headlines, and brought the St. Augustine movement to the forefront. In June, Dr. Martin

Luther King, Jr. was arrested in St. Augustine, and he sent his famous "Letter from the St. Augustine Jail" to Rabbi Israel Dresner in New Jersey, recruiting further support that ended in the mass arrest of American rabbis who conducted a pray-in outside the Monson Motel, where King had been arrested.

In Mississippi, Freedom Summer happened in 1964, during which activists came to the state and the Ku Klux Klan killed, arrested, and harassed blacks to keep them from registering to vote. Of the 17,000 blacks who tried to register, 1,600 succeeded. Despite the relatively small number of registered voters, Freedom Summer did have an impact on the course of the movement, and on July 2, 1964, President Johnson signed the Civil Rights Act of 1964.

President John F. Kennedy and Vice President Lyndon B. Johnson meet with organizers of the March on Washington. Left to right: Willard Wirtz; Floyd McKissick; Mathew Ahmann; Whitney M. Young, Jr.; Dr. Martin Luther King, Jr.; John Lewis; Rabbi Joachim Prinz; Reverend Eugene Carson Blake; A. Philip Randolph; President Kennedy; Vice President Johnson; Walter P. Reuther; Roy Wilkins. White House Photographers; John F. Kennedy Library

Leaving Mississippi and working in Florida

I t took my Mom three attempts to get out of Mississippi. The first time she left Mississippi in the fall of 1963, she went with her brother and five other men in a truck. There wasn't much money, but she sent back about $10 every other week. She had left us in the shotgun house that was almost next to my grandparents' house. She made sure we had coal for the stove; this gave us heat for the winter so we could cook. Our grandparents took care of us and looked out for us, as did our aunts, uncles, neighbors, and friends. We were well taken care of. The older siblings looked after the little ones. We survived it all; our Mom had taught us how to look out for each other.

While she was there, she met a man, Zed. He had a job working for the county as a garbage man. This was considered a very good job because it paid so well. Besides the money, garbage workers would bring things home for the family such as discarded clothes, furniture, and sometimes even food from the white neighborhoods. With his help, my Mom was able to send a little more money back home to help us.

In January 1964, South Florida had a bad freeze and a lot of the crops were destroyed, and Mom had to come back to Mississippi—but in the two months she was in Florida, she had saved enough money to come back and pay off her debts.

In 1965, the second time Mom left Mississippi to go back to South Florida, I remember the night she gathered us all around and told us she was leaving. It was dark in the house; the only thing we could see were the shadows on the wall from the lamp that was burning. That's when she told us she would be going back to Florida. She told us not to worry, that she would come back to get us. I can't tell you the fear I felt—at that time, many people were leaving Sunflower because it was so hard to make a living there. People were leaving their kids with friends and relatives and then not coming back for them. I was afraid Mom wouldn't come back. So I did what I always did when I felt sad: I went up on the roof and cried and sang.

Mom had to sneak out because she didn't want my grandparents to know she was leaving. My grandmother would have done all she could to stop her. Sunday night, she packed up her things and got up early Monday morning as if she was going to work. She put her suitcase on a pickup truck, and when they got to the road crossing at the truck stop, she grabbed her suitcase and got off the truck. She was in Morehead, about a block from the Greyhound station. Mom was afraid someone was following her, so she tried very hard to stay out of sight. She went into a hair shop and had her hair done, hid in the bathroom, and waited for the Greyhound bus. When she got on the bus heading for Florida, that's when her fears went away.

Mom arrived in Homestead, Florida late that night, and the next day was the Fourth of July. She told me that when she arrived about 2 a.m. it was very dark, and she had to walk all the way to the Golden Nugget, where Zed had told her he had a room for the two of them. Mom was afraid to walk on the side streets, so she walked straight down Front Street, which is four streets down from the main street in Homestead.

When she got to Golden Nugget and knocked on the door, someone came out and told her that Zed was in jail. She was totally destroyed. She had no place to stay, but someone who knew Zed came around the corner. She said she could take Mom to J.R. and Margaret's house—they were from Sunflower, our hometown! These people charged my Mom $5 a week for rent. She worked very hard, paid them their rent, and saved money to send back home to help us.

One day, after working hard in the fields all day, she came home and found the door locked. J.R. and Margaret had been thrown out. Once again she had no place to stay, but the rent man knew that she was a hard worker and had been paying her rent on time. It turned out they were not being fair to her and hadn't been paying the rent to him, so he had to put them out. He honored her $5 a week room, and Mom said she felt so happy because she still had a place of her own.

There was another big freeze later that year, and she had a hard time making money. The only work she could get was clean-up in the fields of all the dead vegetables on the ground; she was paid $12 a day.

Later in the same year (1965), Mr. L.C., the bus driver who drove the migrant worker bus bringing people out of Mississippi, was the same bus driver who would take people to work in the fields to pick tomatoes, beans, and limes. One day, he announced in Mom's field that he was leaving to go to Mississippi to pick up a load of people and asked if anyone wanted to come. The cost was $75, and my Mom said she wanted to go to pick up her children. She had only $50 and promised to pay him the rest later.

My Mom arrived in Mississippi on a Friday and she worked for two days—Friday night and Saturday—getting all of us children ready to come with her back to Florida. She washed and combed hair for two nights, gave us baths, and made sure we had food for the whole trip to Florida. They put us all in the back of the bus. Mom was the only one who had kids, and there were eight of us. I still remember getting on the bus looking back at those cotton fields disappearing behind us, and seeing that old house I was born in off Highway 49W. My twin used to see an imaginary lady sitting on bags of cotton and she said goodbye to her.

By the time we got to Florida, Zed was out of jail, and he met us near Fourth Street, where the bus dropped off people coming from Mississippi. My Mom said that Zed was thrilled when the bus got there. When the first child came off, he was all smiles; the second child came off and he was still smiling. Even when the third child came off he was smiling. After the fourth child came off the bus, his smiles started to change. When the fifth child came off, his smile turned into a frown. The sixth child came off and he was looking sad; the seventh child came off and there were tears in his eyes. When the last child came off, the man began to cry. My Mom said she'd told him she had this many kids, but he didn't believe her. (She actually had nine by this time—Clayborne, her first child born when she was 14, had been taken to be raised by her parents.)

He was not the type of man who would hit a woman; he showed his anger in other ways. When he got upset, he would cut up the furniture or cut up her clothes. When she got mad at him, she did the same—she would burn his clothes and just rocked as they burned, although she would not burn his work clothes.

My Mom had one child with Zed, my baby sister Wanda. After that, she did not have any more children.

That is the only time I remember my grandmother coming to Florida—my Mom became very sick after she had her last child. They tied her tubes in the hospital. Six months later, she went back to the hospital because she was having some major problems. She was swelling up, so they had to go in and remove everything. Mom couldn't work in the fields any more—no longer could she pick up the pail of tomatoes or hampers of beans.

Before this, when she first brought us to Florida from Mississippi, she worked hard every day in the fields to the point that she had a nervous breakdown. She would have to take a break and go on the bus because she was trembling and nervous and couldn't keep working. Her nerves were completely down.

Zed stayed with Mom until my baby sister was about two years old. Their relationship turned really bad during the time of her pregnancy. He said something to her that brought back a lot of bad memories of things that happened to her when she was a child. My sister and I were about 13 when he asked my Mom if she would let him have one of us, since she couldn't do anything. This made my Mom very sick and she turned against him completely. Their relationship was destroyed—she did not trust or believe in him anymore.

After my Mom couldn't work in the fields, she wasn't sure what to do to take care of us. In South Florida, there were a lot of people who had come from Mississippi and other states. Some did not read or write; they only knew how to work in the fields. There were a lot of single mothers, and most of them had many kids, as my Mom did. In the state of Florida, if it got to the point where a person couldn't work in the fields, they could get help from the state. Welfare most of the time was not given to a single person, but if you had children they would definitely help. She didn't know she could get welfare, because back in Mississippi, they said she was an unfit mother because she had so many kids from so many different fathers. In Mississippi they wouldn't give it to her, so when she got to Florida she didn't apply for it. Luckily, my Mom was assigned a social worker who helped put her on welfare.

Mom started working in the Florida Keys in hotels, doing maid work. There was a person they would pay to take them down to the Keys to work in the hotels; they would work from Key Largo to Key West. Mom would leave before daybreak in the morning and get back home at night. A friend of hers, Ms. Eve Mae, would look out for us. This lady was much younger than my Mom, and she was from our hometown. Mom said young people always liked to be around her, and Eve Mae could have been one of her daughters. Whether Mom went to work or not, this is the person who took care of us. Eve Mae was a free spirit and a big drinker, so we got away with lots of things.

After working in the Keys for a while, Mom met a man from Miami, and she got a job cooking in a hospital there. She moved in with him so she could be close to her work. Mom would leave us in Homestead and come back on weekends to make sure we had food and were taken care of. With Eve Mae being such a free spirit and not tough on us, this was a very bad mix for my sister and me; we were about 14 or 15 at the time.

Two of Mom's children had serious medical problems. My sister, Lily C., who was next to us, had seizures. In Mississippi we always had to look out for her. When she would fall out, someone would catch her and put something in her mouth to keep her from choking. My sister didn't get the help she needed until we moved to Florida. She was about 10 years old when we moved to Florida, and for most of those ten years she suffered with seizures with no medical help.

One of my brothers had been born with asthma, and in Mississippi, many nights my Mom would cry on her knees praying to God because my brother couldn't breathe. God answered her prayers, because it came to her one night to boil some hot water and put his head over it so the steam could open him up. This worked, so every time he couldn't breathe this is what she did. When we moved to Florida, his asthma became worse—thank God we were put on welfare, as he was able get the medical help he needed. My Mom was told that the Florida climate is very hard on people with asthma.

Unfortunately, the welfare was a two-edged sword, as it also led to my "medical" treatment of the insertion of the Dalkon Shield around this time and my resulting sterility later.

Anyhow, at the age of 14, my brother was very tall and told people he was older so he could get into the Job Corps. He was accepted, which was a blessing for him—in fact, we believe it saved his life. While in training in the Job Corps, kids are placed with different families. Mom's prayers were answered again—my brother was placed in the state of Washington with a family that accepted him as their own. He stayed with this family for years. The woman, Ms. Mable, treated him like he was her own son, and his asthma just about went away.

My other brother, who was about 18, was working for a man who wanted to have sex with him. My brother told my Mom what this man was trying to do. She went to the man and told him if he tried to put his hands on her child again, she would kill him. My brother quit that job.

We came to South Florida on a margin worker bus, the same bus that would take us to the fields to pick tomatoes, beans, limes, okra—all kinds of fruits and vegetables for the next three to four years. When my Mom took us from Mississippi to Florida, my life was in for a big change, not only in what type of work we did, but how hard black people were on each other. Back home we just worried about how to keep food on the table, and how to stay out of the white folks' way. Homestead was a cutthroat place where black people killed each other on a daily basis. On the weekends, the killings seemed to double.

In Mississippi working in the cotton fields, life was different from working in the fields in South Florida. One thing was, we didn't have the boss man over our shoulder, we were our own boss. The work was piece work, which means that you were paid by the bucket or hamper of fruit or vegetable you picked. You were paid 50 cents for a bucket of tomatoes, and for a hamper of beans, 75 cents. They would weigh it—you had to have so many pounds. Some people would try to fool the men who were doing the weighing by putting rocks in the hamper, but most of the time they didn't get away with this.

Most of the people were migrant workers, people who came from different states—Mississippi, Georgia, Alabama, California—these were people who did season work. When the crops were finished in Florida, they would go to other places like Washington state to pick apples, or Georgia to pick peaches. Most of those workers were Mexicans and African-Americans. People don't know there were a lot of black people in South Florida working in those fields. The work consisted of picking all kinds of beans, vegetables, and fruits. Back in the '60s a lot of produce came from that area.

When it came to working in those fields, you had to know what kind of clothes to wear; you could hurt yourself. Most of the time you had to wear long sleeves and gloves, because that stuff could eat you up, especially the leaves from the okra. The same thing working the citrus groves—a lot of those trees had thorns on them. If you didn't know how to pick the fruit and avoid sticking yourself, you could get a nasty cut. Back home picking cotton, we had to be very careful getting the cotton out of the boll because the boll had four or five thorns surrounding the cotton. Another dangerous plant called Johnson grass was sharp like a razor blade; if you were to accidentally swipe it across your hand, it would give you a very deep cut.

Another thing I hated was the little green tree frogs in the lime groves. They were the same color as the leaves on the trees, so you couldn't see them. One person would go up the ladder and pull the limes down, and the person on the ground would pick them up and put them in the bucket. When we worked, the frogs were everywhere.

Early one morning, I was up in a lime tree. Dew was on the ground and on the trees. A frog jumped on my neck—I can still feel that cold, wet frog on my neck today just thinking about it. I ran like a bat out of hell.

Working in the bean fields gave us a good yield if we got a field that had the second pick—that was when the most beans were on the vine. They were called string beans if they were hung on a string for them to grow, and pole beans if they were put on poles, where they would grow up to about four feet tall. I hated working those fields, because sometimes you would reach to pick a bunch of beans and there would be a snake under the bean stalk. When people saw a snake, they would holler "Snake!" I would just get sick, because every time I would put my hand down to get a handful of beans, I just knew a snake was there. I became quite fearful.

We lived in a duplex, a family of eight or nine on each side; we had two rooms and a kitchen for all of us. This was better than Mississippi, though, because we had a toilet inside, and hot and cold water. We would get up very early in the morning to go to the corner to catch the bus that went to the fields. On our way to work, most of the kids were very sleepy, and on the way home, the grownups would gamble once they had they a little money. We would stop at the store for food, drinks, beer and wine, and some people would play games like keno, cards, or dice on the floor in the back of the bus. That Florida sun was hot just like the Mississippi sun, but I could handle it better. You had to pack a lunch to take to the field; most of the time there wasn't much food for lunch for us kids. We would go back to the bus and steal other people's food. If people found out that someone was taking their lunch, they would say that they were going to put poison in the food. I found out the hard way it wasn't poison, but something that kept me in the bushes all day.

When we went to work, there were always some drunks on the bus—working the fields, they would make just enough money to keep the wine flowing. We called them winos. They would start the day with a bottle of Thunderbird or MD 20/20. All through the day they would stay drunk. Some of these men were very nice and good-looking. I didn't understand why they drank like that. When I look back, some of the stuff these men were carrying had to be very heavy on them and the only release they got was through drinking. Some of them had to leave their whole family knowing they would never see them again, and some had to do whatever they could to get away from Mississippi and other places. Lots of these men, and some women, you never got to know because they just would not talk. Most of them went to their graves with this pain, never to let it go.

Most of the women I looked up to at that age were hard-working women and hard drinkers. I knew about five or six who drank themselves into early graves. One lady we used to call Snook would wake up in the morning with a beer in her hand and go to bed at night with a beer in her hand. She got to the point where she couldn't work; her son and friend would keep her supplied with beer. One morning they found her dead in her bed with beer cans all around her. Something was very sad about her, and no one ever found out what was going on. Just like the men, she was one of many casualties. I started drinking at a very early age, around 14. Back then, sweet wines were made in all kinds of flavors—apple, grape, pineapple. I think this stuff was just to attract the kids. It sure got me.

At this time I got to meet some new people including Mexicans. Most of them were migrant workers. Lots of the Mexicans and black people lived in labor camps, and there were some mean people in those camps who would kill you in a minute. Most of them were hiding from the law—people who ran away from Mississippi or other places, because of something they had done. There was a club called Bucket of Blood where, after working all week, people would go hang out, get drunk, and kill somebody. There was a killing every weekend, because some man was looking at another man's woman, or looking at each other and saying things like "If you look at me one more time I will cut your throat"—and they would.

The black women were the same way. Everybody carried a knife, or potash that they would throw on you and it would eat your face off. God only knows what was in it. All I knew was, it could kill you or cripple you for life.

There were killings among black men and women who were lovers. One young lady was a good friend of my Mom's; she was very pretty and kind to me. One night she went out with another man, and her boyfriend found out and strangled her right by our back door. Another time was with a lady who lived in front of us. Mrs. Mattie Mae had a husband, and when her husband went to work, she had a boyfriend who came to her house. Her husband came home early one day and killed this man—he had told this man to stay away from his house. The man was walking out of his house with a slice of bread in his mouth. He killed him right there with that bread in his mouth—I saw this—and they let that man lie there all night.

The grownups didn't care what the little black kids were looking at or listening to. This has stayed with me all my life. This is something that came from slavery when the kids had to watch all kinds of hanging, burning, lynching, all of this to keep them in line. So black people never thought about what this would do to a child's mind and they didn't care.

The man I thought I loved

After moving to Florida when I was 13, my life went crazy. Boys started taking advantage of me and introduced me to wine and beer.

I hated going to school because of the way the kids would treat you just because you dressed differently or had dark skin and were from Mississippi. Most of them were from Georgia, Alabama, or other states. When you said you were from Mississippi, you were mud, someone to be picked on. When my family moved from South Dade to Miami, for years I wouldn't tell people I was from Mississippi. It is another reason why I started singing the blues late—I was ashamed of it, and just wouldn't sing it.

Black boys in those days seemed like they hated black girls. They formed groups that would go around, and any girl they saw walking down the street, day or night, they would grab you and pull you into their car and have their way with you. They would run what they called a "train" on a girl; this means they would stand in line and each boy would have sex with you. This would go on until they got tired.

In school there is always some person who just doesn't like you. One person I called Cockeye Susie just wanted to beat the hell out of me. Cockeye Susie kept telling me she was going to beat my butt. One day after school, she was ready for me. To get from school to my house, there was a big field we had to cross and she was going to meet me in that field. Cockeye Susie had been telling me all day that she wanted to meet me after school in the field.

When a fight was about to jump off, kids would crowd around and make a big circle that you couldn't get out of. All day long I was in fear of the last school bell ringing. As I walked out of the school building, I didn't see Cockeye Susie. I started feeling good—maybe she had changed her mind, and I surely hoped so. However, when I got to the field, Cockeye Susie sprang up with a bunch of other kids. Before I knew it, I was in this circle with Cockeye Susie popping me upside my head. Every time I would try to get out, someone would push me back in.

When you are a coward, you figure out ways to get out of things. I walked on top of some people's heads and got out of there. I made it home, never to go back to school again. To tell the truth I liked school, but I let someone bully me and thus changed the course of my whole life.

My twin sister was a fighter, though. I remember one time Fat Sally, who was a little older and worked in the fields with us, came to our house one evening. For some reason she wanted to beat us all up. My Mom was working in Miami at the time, and no grownup was there. Fat Sally was downstairs, calling us all kinds of names, blabbing what she was going to do to us. My sister got a knife, went downstairs, walked right up to Fat Sally, stabbed her, and let all the air out of her. Fat Sally ran. Later, when the police came to the house, my sister told them what happened. Nothing was done, and we never had any more problems from her. To this day Fat Sally has great respect for my sister. Every time she would see me, she would ask, "Where is that mean old sister of yours?"

Drinking was a way of trying to get your mind off of what was going on around you. I used to wonder what was going on with those winos and so many others who were into alcohol. Once I started drinking, I realized what it could do. It gave me false courage, and it eased the pain of life. There were a lot of women who drank themselves to death; I knew three. One lady drank beer every waking hour. I used to love going to her house; that is one of the places where I first drank. The beer was Colt 45 malt liquor, which was a very strong beer—other beers were not so strong. Later on I moved to wine—sweet, cheap wines are very appealing to kids. One of them was Boone's Farm, which makes all kinds of flavors including apple, strawberry, and lime. Other wines like Mogen David, 20-20, and Thunderbird are the ones winos like.

I never got a taste for them. I was a very bad drinker and would not stop until I was knocked out. I would be sick for two or three days, and start all over again. Thank God that back then I was not introduced to hard drugs; I'm sure if I was, I probably would have gotten caught up in that too.

Sex is something I was never taught about. It became something I was ashamed of. I couldn't understand what the big deal was, or why boys and men were so crazy over it.

I found this slick-talking boy that I liked, and I thought he liked me. I would go to his house, where we would drink beer and wine and listen to music. One day he asked me to go with him to a friend's house, and I did. When I walked in, it was dark. He turned on the light—there were four or five other boys there, and I froze. What they did to me I could not say because I left my body. The next thing I remember was being dropped off about four blocks from my house. I was in pain all over and I never told anyone. This went on with the same boys a few more times. I would be playing in the yard, and they would drive by and call me to get into the car, and I would. I was so ashamed and filled with fear; I thought no one would believe me.

Years later, I asked Mom if she knew the things that were going on with me. She told me there were many nights she heard me screaming and hollering in my sleep, telling someone to stop, to leave me alone. She was so hurt for me but didn't know what to do, because I wouldn't talk.

Once I was on my way home when a car pulled up next to me and somebody tried to pull me into the car. I ran like hell. There was an old couple sitting on the porch—I ran to them and asked them to help me. Somebody in the car told them I was his wife and for them to send me down. This old man and his wife looked at me and told me I should go to my husband; my heart sank. I ran into their house, straight to the kitchen, and grabbed a knife. I saw the back door and ran out and got home safely. A few days later, I went to the couple's house and I told them what was going on that night, and gave them back their knife. Back then they didn't have the laws for messing with an underage child and for rape like they do now.

In the arms of the black man, I became a tool to be used and abused. I was still looking for love from the men who came into my life. Without a father figure in my life, I kept looking for that. Going about it the wrong way, I paid a big price.

Sammy the Whammy was about 5 feet 4 and he had five brothers. Years earlier, his family had moved from Mississippi to South Florida. They were all short men; some of their ancestors had to be from the African pygmy tribes. Sammy the Whammy carried the label they put on black men; I paid the price because he was tearing up my body inside.

Sammy the Whammy became my warrior and my protector; I looked up to him as a father figure and lover wrapped up in one. Sammy the Whammy was very kind to me. I was about 15, he was around 30, and I was crazy about him. He had a black and white Thunderbird with the fish tail on the back—I would see this car coming and damn near pee myself. The man would tell me to go home and I would not—I just wanted to be with him. The things I took my Mom through with this man I regret today and have begged her to forgive me. Once, she came and beat me out of his bed and took me to the field to pick limes. She even went and talked to him about me; he told her he had tried to get me to go home but I wouldn't. I guess I was getting some kind of love and didn't want to let it go.

With Sammy the Whammy, if anyone would bother with me, he would go to them and have a talk and they would leave me alone. I felt protected by him. Life felt good. He lived in a trailer park. He would let me go down to the store and get what food I wanted to eat on credit, and at the end of the week he would pay for it. At home with Mom, there were still times when the food ran a little short, and with him there was no one else to compete with for things.

This guy had other women who liked him and wanted to be with him. I didn't care as long as I was staying in his trailer, having plenty of food, and he came home to me.

One night, I went out and I found out just how badly some of the women wanted him, and wanted me out of the picture. I went to the Bucket of Blood club, where we were just hanging out. This was one of those weekends when everybody was drinking, bumping and grinding, and eating the best fish sandwiches in town. I was in the bar, had my Colt 45, and was listening to some blues. I was one of those people who didn't like to fight, but with a few drinks in me I became someone else. The beer gave me false courage.

I got up to go to the bathroom and I was looking in the mirror, when someone shouted for me to look out. I turned around and a girl was coming at me with a straight razor. I grabbed her by the arm she had the razor in, and pushed her to the floor. Somehow, I got her over to one of the toilet stalls and put her head and wig into the toilet. After that, the group and I went outside to leave the club. We were standing out back getting ready to leave, when here came this woman at me again! A friend who was with me put something into my hand; I pointed it at her and she froze. She left me and my sweet Sammy the Whammy alone. I wanted to be his only fool.

Then one day things came to a halt. Sammy the Whammy made me go home. He became very mean to me. He said he didn't want me any more and his wife was coming back. He had never said anything to me about a wife. His wife had been in the crazy house and she was coming home.

My whole world fell apart. For days I didn't know what to do. I wanted this man and I wanted him bad. I was out of my head; I would go and hang around the trailer park just to get a look at him. One day I went off the deep end and went to talk to her. I asked her if we could share him. This lady could have killed me and not do a day in jail, because of her condition. She said to me that this man wasn't worth it, that I was young and needed to forget about him, and that would be the best thing for me.

Sammy the Whammy was the first person I fell in love with and really the first man I *agreed* to have sex with. My life was through at that time. Everything started falling apart around me. My twin sister was a fighter—she would have cut his balls off. You did her wrong, she would get back at you somehow or some way, whatever it took. Not me. I hated fighting; I was a coward and very afraid. I would go in some corner and cry and feel sorry for myself.

Around this time, a group of girls was trying to double-team my sister. I was sitting on the stairs when my Mom tried to get me up to help her, but I couldn't move.

That's when they all started calling me crazy again. I thought my whole family had turned on me.

That was the day I decided to end it all. I made plans of what I was going to do with everything I could find in the bathroom. I even drank some bleach. Afterward, I went into the kitchen where they were all sitting around being happy. I sat at the table, not saying anything. The next thing I remember we were at the hospital, and my head hurt and I was sore all over. I was taken home and never got any kind of therapy; back then, they just didn't do that for black people. We took care of it ourselves, just kept on drinking.

While writing this, I called my Mom. She said she should have gotten me some help. My Mom did what she was taught—to keep on moving—saying "This, too, shall pass."

Looking back on what I went through as a young girl, I wanted someone to love me, but I didn't know what love was. What I have discovered is you must first learn to love yourself. This is something I wasn't taught: how to love myself. We do not come into life knowing this, and we must be taught by our Mom, Dad, and the people who are around us. This is something that was taken from us during slavery. We were not allowed to care for each other because your life did not belong to you.

There's no reason for us to carry this kind of thinking with us today. You are in charge, and you know who you are. *That* is why so many people were so mean to me—because I didn't love myself and I let them treat me the way they did. I didn't have the courage at that time to stand up for myself.

Another black girl gone wild

After trying to get out of life, which didn't work, I just got wild. I started hanging out in those juke joint junk places like the Blue Moon, Dew Drop Inn, Bucket of Blood. People didn't ask about your age—as long as you had the money to pay for your drink, you were in. If you didn't have the money, some guy would get it for you for a quickie in the back seat of his car or in the bushes. They might even buy you a sandwich if you were real good.

Another juke joint in town was Mom's Café. This was one of those places they called a hole in the wall. It had sawdust on the floor, and people would be bumping and grinding and just having a good time. Always, some drunk who had been working all week and just got paid, knocked himself out in the corner and pissed all over himself. He didn't make it home with his paycheck and his wife didn't catch him in time.

But Mom's Café was different. You didn't fight in her club, you did your fighting and killing outside.

I remember one night at Mom's Café, my friend Sweet Pete got killed. I had always admired Sweet Pete—he was a very handsome man and he treated me like I was his sister. A fight started with him and some other man. They were told to take it outside. He went outside and went to the trunk of his car, and when he went to open his trunk, the other man pulled out a gun and blew him away.

Most of the time, before the police got there, everyone would disappear. No one would come forward and say who did it. This man got away with it. A lot of the killings that went on down there, they could never prove who did it. People would leave town and that was it. I went deeper and deeper into a world of not caring; I had no shame and didn't care. One reason I liked drinking was that it would give me false courage. I would get drunk and pretend I was someone else most of the time. But I was stoned out of my head. I was just 15 and didn't know what this stuff was doing to my brain and body.

School? Who in the hell wanted to go to school? Most of the time the kids were making fun of me or wanted to fight. I started skipping school to hang out at some older people's houses all day. (When I say older, I'm talking about people who were not school age.)

One time when I was playing hooky, I was riding someone's bike when a car came from out of nowhere and knocked me off the bike. My left leg got caught up in the back tire, and I had to have a cast on that leg for about three months. I still have pain in that leg today. The older I get, the more pain it gives me. I guess that's pay-back.

That is when Mom found out that I wasn't going to school. Mom had to slow her life down, because she had two teenage twin girls who were giving her hell. She said once a lady came to her and told her that the only reason she didn't kill one of us is because we were Mom's children. My sister and I didn't hang out much together—she had her friends and I had mine.

The men in my sister's life were very kind to her, except for one man I called Tall Tom. Mary moved in with him; when he went to work, he would lock her up in the house. I remember many times I went over there and had to talk to her through the bathroom window.

One of the things that was so bad about him was that he was a married man. One day his wife went to Mom, carrying a gun in her hand, blabbing that she was going to kill Mary. Mom got on her knees and begged this lady not to kill her child—she said to kill her instead.

After this, my Mom went to Tall Tom's house pleading for Mary to come home. However, every time Mary would move to come to her, Tom would reach into his pocket as if he had a gun. For about 45 minutes, Mom pleaded but she gave up because Mary was too afraid to leave. Eventually Mary was able to escape, and never went back—but Mom found out that Tom had told Mary that if she had left that day he would have killed her. After Tall Tom went back to his wife, he killed her! He said it was self-defense, but he did some time in prison. When he came out of prison, he looked very strange and he never was the same.

Once my sister ran away. I went looking for her, but when I found her, I stayed where she was. We were just 15 miles from Homestead. When my Mom came looking for us, someone told us she was outside. We jumped out of the window, got into someone's car, and took off. She was behind us, and somebody was shooting at the car.

Looking back, it seemed like forever, but it wasn't—it was a very short time between the age of 12 and 17. We went crazy.

This had to come to an end, and it did.

When I did go back home, Mom opened the door and let me in, but the next thing I knew the police were knocking on the door. When I saw them, I pushed past them and ran out the door. This big old cop was on my tail—when he caught me, I kicked this man so hard in between his legs that it pains me today to think of it— wherever you are, please forgive me for that.

After that, I was sent to reform school. I really liked the place—I had my own room, nice clean clothes to wear, plenty of food, and they took us to some nice places. I was going to school in peace there, having fun with no one pick on me. When it came time for me to go, I didn't want to leave, but I had done my time and had to. If I'd been in a place like this when I first came from Mississippi, I believe my life would have been different.

Mom was still working in Miami, and she decided to move us there. When we moved, I never did go back to school. I started doing factory work, and didn't do so much drinking. I was all right for a while. I worked in one factory where we made box springs for beds, and one place where we made all kinds of boxes. I worked in a factory that made orange juice, grapefruit juice, and fruit cocktail.

Miami was very good when it came to helping people with little or no education. I even went to trade school for billing and maintenance. In this school I learned how to wire up electricity to a whole house and was taught how to do all kinds of plumbing.

Miami was different from Homestead—it had more class,

and less killing. I found out that I had a lot going for me and I wanted to learn more. At this time I was trying to take over my own life, and not let someone else live it for me.

Sometimes when it seems everything is all right, and you say, "I've got this!" life can throw you a blow to see if you really do have it. At this time I was still very young, around 17, and it already felt as if I had been to hell and back. Evidently life was preparing me for what was to come.

Overtown

In Miami, in the factories we did piece work—we got paid based on how many items we turned out. In that way, it was similar to working in the tomato fields. One thing I did learn from my Mom was how to work.

I was very good at finding a job—but I wasn't very good at keeping one. I would get my pay and want to move on. And, I was still under age and doing things I shouldn't have been doing, like working in a club as a barmaid. I always looked older—when I was 17, people took me for around 22. I was always the one to get the party started, and the first to fall out drunk. I could drink and then fall asleep anywhere.

Truthfully, I didn't like the taste of alcohol, I just liked the way it made me feel. I would drink it down fast. It went to my head fast, and I was out like a light. Later I realized that I was using drinking as a medication, trying to numb all the pain.

Miami is where I got introduced to marijuana; call it pot, weed, reefer, Mary Jane, whatever—I was into it. I remember one day I was sitting outside puffing on a joint. It was raining lightly, and I could see every little raindrop. I was at peace with the world and everything in it.

Miami was much different from Homestead. Miami had some very nice clubs—they weren't juke joints, and not much killing went on. One club that we called Under the Tree had a huge parking lot with trees lined up and down the parking lot. It was like a big horseshoe, with one way in and one way out. When you drove in, people were everywhere, some in cars and some sitting in chairs under the trees. People would drive through this circle very slowly, as if they were in a parade. Whenever a car came through, all eyes were on that particular car until it parked or left. Those brothers and sisters made sure they had their cars in the best of shape and looking good. Everyone was checking out everyone else.

Way before you got to the place, you could smell the smoke from the barbecue and the scent of the fried fish and chicken in the air. There were vendors everywhere selling all kinds of things—vegetables, fresh fish, clothes—you name it, they had it. This place would be jam-packed, especially on Sunday. People would come out dressed to impress, from their clothing to their hair processes.

Most of the people would just sit in their cars in the parking lot. Sometimes people would go inside and get a table so they could play the jukebox and dance. Outside, there was always someone playing some sweet sounds from their car. Inside or out, it was a good time for all. They had a package store where you could get liquor with some ice to go—any kind of liquor you wanted, they had it. There was always someone in the parking lot who'd just brought in some moonshine from Georgia or Alabama, selling it by the shot. You could have liquor, wine, beer, or moonshine, and just enjoy watching people coming and going.

This place had everything party people wanted: plenty of men and women, and a lot of sex going on in those cars. Sometimes on the weekends they would have live music; it was good, and there was a cover charge. You could go inside where they had the air conditioning on, get in a dark corner, and make out with somebody's husband or wife. For some reason, I can't recall much hell breaking out in this place. I think a cop was the owner, I'm not sure—but the place was very well maintained. You had to have ID to get into the club; someone was at the door checking. Of course there's always someone who can make a false ID for you. Every time someone makes a rule, someone figures out a way to break it.

There was a lot of work for black women in Miami Beach as maids in people's houses or working in hotels. I had a few jobs doing maid service in some of the hotels. Once, I was a night maid, cleaning up behind people, and if someone wanted anything—extra towels or sheets—I had to be there to take it to them.

However, if you were black and worked on the Beach at night, you couldn't leave until the next morning. Back in the late '60s and early '70s, it was still the law that if you were black and went to Miami Beach, you had to have a certain ID showing that you were working there. A black person could not be found on the street after a certain time, or else you could go to jail—but that was still better than back in Mississippi, where you might be found in the bottom of the river wrapped up in chains.

Back then, an area called Overtown, a neighborhood in Miami, was The Place for big-time black entertainers who came to perform in Miami Beach. They couldn't stay on the Beach, so they would come to Overtown to stay, play, and party.

Josephine Baker and friends in Knightbeat Club at the Sir John Hotel. Photo: The Black Archives History & Research Foundation of South Florida, Inc.

Overtown started out as a black settlement. The city of Miami was incorporated in 1896, and black and brown immigrants from Cuba, the Caribbean, and other places, including Mississippi, settled into their own segregated community known as Colored Town. Soon, businesses started moving in including shops and clubs, and it became a center of late-night black entertainment known as Overtown.

In its heyday, Overtown's legendary performers included Josephine Baker, Cab Calloway, Nat "King" Cole, Sammy Davis, Jr., Ella Fitzgerald, Redd Foxx, Aretha Franklin, and Billie Holiday. They performed on the "Little Broadway" strip that was on Second Avenue and is now long gone.

When I was there in the '60s and early '70s, most of the Overtown clubs were still black-owned, or else a black person was fronting for a white person. Overtown had the Sir John Club, the Hampton House, Mr. James Club, and the Mary Elizabeth Hotel. Most of the clubs had gone out of business by the time I was there. But I did catch the tail end of things.

Deceived again and again

I was still having a bad time trying to find a man. I met one who said he liked me and off I went again. This man lived in a rooming house and I spent a lot of time in his room. He would leave me and go spend time with a married woman when her husband would go to work. He was very mean to me, calling me names, beating on me, and all I would do was cry. One night, I was in his bed; someone knocked on the door and told me that he had been shot and was in the hospital. That lady's husband had come home, caught him with his wife, and shot him. I went every day to see him in the hospital, and when he came home, I treated him like a baby—I took good care of him, even giving him baths. I should have been mad, but I wasn't—I was just glad to be there for him. After all my good treatment, when that man got back on his feet he went straight back to that woman. Her husband went to jail and he got the man's wife. He was there with her for about three babies and left her.

It took another man to bring me down real bad. I lost all trust in men and just about all people, from what this man did to me. I was working as a barmaid when I met Slick Nick. This guy would come around the bar and try to get me to go to his house. I told him no, but he kept on trying. One night I said yes. He picked me up and took me to his house; when we got there, he gave me this big joint of reefer while he went to take a shower. I lit the joint—the smoke was kind of hard to pull out, and it had a fumy smell, but I still tried to smoke it.

Whatever that guy gave me that night was something I wasn't used to; it was very strong. I found out later that this guy worked in the shipyard, where he had access to some heavy-duty stuff. I was used to the light stuff around town. I kept puffing on that joint, finally getting some smoke. Soon I started feeling kind of funny—I got up and went into the bathroom, where he was taking a bath. This freaked me out, because he'd told me he was going to take a shower.

I went back into the living room and sat down. I didn't like the way I was feeling. I was getting too high, and I wanted to come down and go home. At the time, I was living with my Mom. I kept thinking that I didn't want her to see me like this. He told me that if we had sex, it would help me to come down.

We tried that, and it didn't work. I pushed him off of me—I just wanted to get out. I put on what clothes I could find and ran for the door. I went down the stairs and got to the street, and then I heard sirens. I was sure it was the law, looking for me. I wanted to escape, but Slick Nick caught up with me, and convinced me to come back upstairs with him. I saw that he was afraid, because if I was found in the street like that, he could go to jail because I was under age. Miami was stricter on people messing with under age children. All the abuse that was going on with young girls in other parts of South Florida wasn't happening in Miami. I told him I would stay until morning—I asked him to turn off the different colored lights, turn off the music, and just turn on the television. The last thing I remembered was Johnny Carson going off. I did calm down and went to sleep. I hated this man for what he did to me, putting something in that reefer just to have sex. This was another man deceiving me and taking advantage of me for no reason. He didn't have to do that—I would have given it up anyway.

My life started to change again. I lost trust in people, and I became afraid and withdrawn, for all the deception had taken its toll.

I had to find out how to change my life. Here I was, still no more than 17 or 18 when my life had fallen apart again.

I started going to church—I found a Holiness Church. I was feeling good about myself—I stopped drinking, smoking, and having sex. I even started a little singing group with the kids in the neighborhood. I would pick them up and bring them to church, and I taught Sunday school. This church was very small and consisted of mostly older people. I was the youngest person there and did everything I could to help the church.

Sometimes I went to the Pastor's house and would help him and his wife at their house. I loved them. The Pastor reminded me of my grandfather. He was helping me and teaching me all kinds of things, for the betterment of the church and me. The house I lived in belonged to one of the women in the church; she believed in a lot of things I didn't understand.

Sometimes in church I would see these people acting very strange—something would come over them and they would shout, shake all over, praise God, and cry. Whatever this was, I wanted it, and I tried very hard to get it. I would go down on my knees and call Jesus's name over and over, but nothing would happen. We would do this for hours, three to four times a week.

I remember the last time I got down on my knees to do this, after about 20 minutes a voice came into my head very clearly and said to get up and get out of this church. And I did.

The woman who was renting the house to me made me move. After about three or four months, I heard that the Pastor was sick. I wanted to go see him, but they wouldn't let me come to see him.

The next thing I heard was that he had passed away. I found out where they were having his service, and I went because I wanted to say goodbye. When I went into the church, the Pastor's wife came to me and told me to leave. She said it was because of me that the Pastor died. I couldn't understand this. I became very guilt-ridden and confused about life and myself, and I went into a very dark hole.

I gave up. I didn't want to do anything other than sleep and cry. Everything was so dark and ugly. I didn't trust anyone.

Then a strange thing started happening. I would be walking down the street and a funny feeling would come over me, a feeling of doom—and I just wanted to run. So I wouldn't go down that street, as if the street was causing this to happen to me. This went on with me for years; it would come and go. I didn't tell anyone because I thought I was losing my mind. It got to the point sometimes even being around people that this would happen. So I would avoid that person or place—wherever I had that feeling, I stayed away. My world started getting smaller and smaller.

I found out later on in life that I was having panic attacks. Back then they didn't have the treatment or the information that is now known about panic attacks. When this feeling came over me, I wanted to run to someplace where I would feel safe. But how can you run from yourself? I was afraid I would start screaming. I had this feeling of doom, and I saw in my mind being put into a straitjacket and being taken away for the rest of my life. If you ever had one, you would know it—the fear would be so intense it became painful. Imagine you are out in the woods, and a grizzly bear was coming at you and there was no place for you to run or hide. This is the type of fear I was having, and there was nothing around me but me. I would look for reasons why this was happening to me, and I started thinking someone was doing this to me and not that I was doing it to myself.

With all of this going on in my mind, another man showed up in my life, Off Track Don. Off Track Don was taking medicine for his nerves. I started taking it too, and I just got worse—all the problems he had, I thought I had them too. But truthfully, Off Track Don had a right to be in the shape he was, because he saw his daughter murdered right in front of his face. He was something I did not need in my life. I think the whole thing I was doing was trying to find someone to lean on so I wouldn't have to take responsibility for myself.

Off Track Don finally went completely off and I really don't know what happened to him next. Years later, when I took a trip back to Miami, I saw him on the streets—he was pushing a shopping cart and going through garbage cans. He was dressed like a bum, the hair on his head and face long and matted down. I spoke to him, but he didn't know who I was.

After the breakup with him, my life was in a complete dark mess. My twin sister was the manager of a rooming house, and she got me a room there. All I wanted to do was stay in that room and listen to Mahalia Jackson and Carole King. Carole King had a song I listened to all the time called "Way Over Yonder," because at the time I just wanted to go away. People tried to get me to go out, but I felt like God had turned his back on me. This room was more like a casket; I was slowly getting ready to take myself out of life completely.

One day, a very strange thing happened. I was going to have what I'd planned to be my last meal; it was a steak and potato that my sister brought to me. I was chewing on a piece of steak, and when I tried to swallow, it got stuck in my throat. No one was around to help me. If I really wanted to die, I would have let that piece of meat take me out, but I fought like hell to get that piece of meat out of my throat. I was pulling and pulling, trying to get this meat out of my throat, and it just would not come out. I remember screaming in my head, "Oh, God, help me!" and that is when it just popped out.

After that, I wanted to live.

One day I did come out of my room and went to my Mom's house. A man was there who she wanted me to meet, a man named Jamaica Frank. He was a very nice person—he was from Jamaica and worked on one of the cruise ships.

Somehow or another, I married him. At that time, when you married someone from another country, after the marriage they went back to their country and you had to sign the final papers to get them back over here. After we were married, he went back to Jamaica and I went back to my little room. I got some pep in me and was just waiting on my Jamaica Frank to return. I had signed all the papers for him and had just one more to sign for him to come over to America to stay as a citizen.

It was one of those beautiful tropical Florida days, when my twin sister Mary came to my room and asked me to go with her for a walk. We decided to walk to Overtown. The rooming house where I lived in wasn't far from Overtown, three miles at the most. We left the house and walked over to Second Avenue, where all those famous clubs used to be. You could see signs, but most of the places were boarded up. There were still a few clubs left, though—the Knightbeat was one. We passed the Knightbeat, and about three blocks down was the famous, even legendary, Mary Elizabeth.

That's when I met him. He was smooth, sweet talking, and good looking. I call him Geechee Fred.

It was in 1971, and I had finally come face to face with the devil.

Geechee Fred

I thought I'd already been through hell in my life, but I was so wrong—it was just getting started. I'd heard people tell stories about Geechee people and how mean they are. When I met this person, I didn't know he was a Geechee from Georgia.

During the years of living with this man, I found out he hated his mother's guts. Any time you run into a man who doesn't like his mother, that is a sign to run and keep running, do not stop. I stayed with this man for 15 years of abuse. When he met me, he saw all the signs and took advantage of them; I was an open book.

He was a damn good looking man, and looking at him, you would never dream of what was lurking inside of this man. The day he met me, he started plotting how he was going to take control of my mind, my body, and even tried to take my soul; but God would not let him take my soul. The Bible in Genesis speaks of how the snake was cunning and crafty and got his way with the woman Eve. That day while walking in Overtown, I met that same snake.

Years later, after I finally got out of the devil's clutches, I did some research on the people they called Geechee from South Carolina, Georgia, and parts of Florida. I wanted to find out exactly what or who I was dealing with at that time in my life.

Before I go any further, let me tell you what I found out about the people they called Geechee. The black people who called themselves Gullah in South Carolina, and Geechee in Georgia (probably because of the name of the Ogeechee River in Georgia), lived in the Lowcountry sea islands, where they were brought by slave traders in the 1500s and later. According to one account, even before slavery ended, the plantation owners fled the Lowcountry—the mosquitoes and diseases such as malaria and yellow fever were too much for them to deal with, although the Gullah/Geechee people tolerated the diseases fairly well. Those who left would appoint certain slaves to be "foremen" over the rice fields. However, another account says the Geechee people ran them off after emancipation.

Either way, left alone to their own devices, the Gullah/Geechee people maintained much of their West African culture and remained isolated, with many of their communities being accessible only by boat. They practiced their Creole-like language, arts and crafts, skills, folklore, culinary traditions, and religious beliefs and rituals that included both voodoo and a form of Christianity based in African mysticism. They were, and are, largely self-sustaining with hunting, farming, and fishing.

Truly, Geechee Fred could have been a great man if he'd only taken the time to find out who he is and where he came from.

The Mary Elizabeth in Overtown is where I met Geechee Fred. As we were walking past, I heard strange music coming out of the place. I had never been to the Mary Elizabeth and didn't even know it was there.

When we peeped in, we saw a very long hallway that was dark. At the end of it, we could see a little bit of light coming through some double doors. Before we got to the end of the hallway, my sister got scared—she told me she wasn't going in there, and we both ran out. If I knew by walking down that hallway and through those double doors how my life was going to change, I would have run and not looked back. But sometimes when life has a plan for you, there is no turning back, and the sound of the music and that lady's voice was drawing me into the place.

I went back, walked down that dark hallway, and went through the double doors. I was shocked at the beauty of the place—there was a big stage with tables and chairs all around it. When I looked to my left, I saw some stairs that led up to a big beautiful bar that had barstools all along it. The place had a dusty, musty smell, as if it had been closed up for a while.

The music I was hearing was coming from the area where the bar was. When I looked a little closer, I saw a man. He was very good looking with a head full of hair. Back then men were using hair processes, and he had his hair processed to the max. I'm talking about the kind of hairdo that James Brown wore—as a matter of fact, he looked a lot like James Brown. The light was very dim, and he didn't see me right away—but when he did, he called for me to come up.

When I got up to where he was, I looked around for where the music was coming from. He was playing an LP record on a turntable. The voice of the woman singing was haunting—it seemed to put me under a spell. He asked me my name, and I told him—and he told me his name. I asked, "Who is that lady singing?" He told me it was Lady Day, Billie Holiday. I fell in love with Lady Day's voice that day.

When I met him I was 18 years old, and for all I had already been through I didn't learn. For the next 15 years I was going to be in a very hard classroom.

After leaving Mississippi and moving to South Florida, I didn't do much singing. We would still sing in the fields, and sometimes on the bus coming home from work. Once I tried to get a little group going called the Grove Girls, but no one was really serious about so it didn't go anywhere.

Back in those days I was very fearful of getting onstage to sing, so my twin was always pushing me up onto the stage to sing. Sometimes, one of the clubs would put on a talent night; you could win money or some other prizes. I never wanted to get up there, I just wanted to sing to myself. My brothers and sisters and I all used to sit on the porch drinking beer and singing to see who could sing the best.

After meeting Geechee Fred, my whole life changed about singing. I wanted to sing like that lady Billie Holiday. I spent the whole evening talking to Geechee Fred, and I completely forgot about my sister. I was fascinated by the things he was telling me and listening to that beautiful music. He told me that he had just come down from New York, that he was running this club for a friend of his, and he was thinking about putting on some talent shows. He asked if I could sing or dance; I told him, a little. Listening to this man talk, I was just blown away about the things he said he had going on in New York. This was my first time meeting someone like this—he looked good, he was a singer, and he acted like he had some money.

When I left the club that night, I was on cloud nine. I had met someone who liked me and wanted to help me. I was so happy! After talking to him that night, I decided I wanted to be a singer and be onstage, and I wanted to sing like that Lady Day, Billie Holiday.

So after that I went to the club every day, listened to Billie singing, and sang along with her. Fred started giving me pointers about singing. I found out he was a great singer himself; he was from the old school of great vocalists like Billy Eckstine, Arthur Prysock, Johnny Hartman. Through him, I was introduced to some great music. I was more into The Supremes, one of the Motown groups that was big at the time. But this music was new to me and I liked it very much.

Geechee Fred was about 20 years older than I was. He was another I looked to as a daddy figure. In writing this book, I'm hoping to help someone—if I don't get anything else out of this book but one thing, please let it be a message to the fathers and Dads, to realize how devastating it is for their daughters when you're not around. A girl needs to have that father figure in her life from the beginning of her life. An older man could be a blessing for a younger woman, or he could be a curse; this was to be my 15 years of living with a curse.

Geechee Fred told me to make sure I came every day so he could help me. He would ask a lot of questions about me, and I started telling him some of the things I'd been through. I told him I had met this guy from Jamaica, we had gotten married, I was waiting for him to come back, and I had one final paper I needed to sign to bring him back into the States.

That is when he told me he believed that somebody had gotten some money for me to marry this guy. He got me thinking that maybe somebody did this because my mind was so bad at the time I wasn't too sure of what I was doing. Geechee Fred convinced me that someone had pulled the wool over my eyes. So I decided not to sign the final paper to bring him back into the States. Geechee Fred convinced me that I was tricked into this marriage.

Then my family started getting upset at me because I was spending so much time with Geechee Fred. They kept trying to get me to come home—but I wouldn't, as I was starting to believe Geechee Fred, who told me that they didn't care. One day, I left Overtown to go see my family. I saw my Mom come out of the

62

grocery store. I went to greet her and tried to give a kiss on her cheek, and she turned her head. That really messed me up.

This is when I decided that Geechee Fred was right: my family did not care for me. I started thinking about the different things that went on in my life and my family. That's when I started putting trust into Geechee Fred and went off track and stayed off for 15 years.

Later on in life, I found out about men like Geechee Fred— one of the first things they do is turn the person against family and friends. And the next thing they do is to isolate you, take you away from them. So the only person you can trust and depend on is them.

This is how most pimps work. They look for young girls or boys who have problems at home. They treat them kindly and show them they are their friend. After they get your trust, they make their move with control of the mind. If that doesn't work, the next step is control with fear. Geechee Fred used all of this on me, and it worked.

As I got to know Geechee Fred, I found out his mother had two sons, him and his brother. She played favorites between them. She would take things from Geechee Fred and give them to his brother, who got the best of everything, because she said one day he was going to be a preacher.

Geechee Fred's brother did grow up to be a big-time preacher and he probably hates his brother to this day. I remember the many phone calls he would make to his brother, telling him how much his mother took from him and gave to his brother.

They called Geechee Fred's mother Geechee Cora. Nobody messed with that woman. She carried a straight razor between her breasts and would cut you in a heartbeat. Bad as things were in those days with black people and white people, they didn't mess with Geechee Cora. Most of the time when white people found a black person like that and they couldn't control them, they would kill them or call them crazy.

He told me about a time when he was a little boy; a white man came to the house threatening her about something. She beat the hell out of him, and nothing was done to her. Years later I got to meet her, and she would always hold her head and constantly complain about headaches. During the time I was with Geechee Fred, at least once a month—after downing a fifth of liquor and whatever else he could get his hands on—he would call her and keep her on the phone for hours talking about what she did to him. What was so sad is that she would stay on the phone and listen to all he had to say. Why she did not hang up on him I do not know; I guess maybe she felt guilty about some of the things she had done to him.

I kept going to the club, listening to Billie Holiday, helping him around the club with cleaning, and working on how he were going to put on a talent show.

One evening I showed up and he asked me, "Girl, do you like me?"

I said yes, and he said, "Do you want to be my girl?"

I said okay. He said, "Okay, go in the back room and take off your clothes and give me some." I really didn't like this guy like that—I just did it because he wanted it and I felt that if I did this he would keep helping me.

Big mistake.

After that, little by little I moved into the club. This is where he was living—he did all his sleeping and cooking in this place that became home for me too.

One night, I got a phone call from my sister, a few months after I'd moved in with Geechee Fred. She told me that my husband, Jamaica Frank, was coming back to Florida. Somehow or another, the last papers got signed and he was coming to the States. I do not recall signing those last papers, but I am so glad they did get signed. I am glad that Frank was able to come into the country, because he turned out to be a blessing; he became a chef.

I regret today that I made the mistake of not staying with Jamaica Frank and going off with a fool instead. I never did see Frank again, and we signed divorce papers in 1978. In this lifetime it was not for me to have it easy; I had some deep dark lessons to learn.

While we were at the club in Overtown, Geechee Fred put on one show, and it was a flop—he made no money from it. After I told him about Jamaica Frank coming back to town, Geechee Fred started making plans of his own about me. He decided that we needed to leave and go back to New York.

One evening, I came to the club and he was just sitting on the stage with his face in his hands. I asked him what was wrong, and he told me that all the money he had was gone, that he couldn't get to the money he had in his bank account in New York, and he had to go back to get the money out. He was in fear that he would lose the place and would have to get out. This left me feeling confused and lost.

He asked me if I knew of anywhere that I could get some money to help us save the club or get back to New York. He remembered me telling him about a few guys I'd messed around with. So he convinced me to try some of these guys and see if they would give me some money. I said, this is something I never did—but he said to me, "You've been giving it away, now you're just trying to get some money to help us save the club and get us to New York. Once we are in New York you will not have to do this."

It started out with me going to a couple of guys I knew, and progressed to picking up men on the street and in bars. He kept telling me that once we were in New York I wouldn't do this any more, and that he was going to help me become a great singer just like Lady Day. I really believed him. I believed him with all my heart and soul. I wanted so badly to get the money so we could go to New York and all of this would be over.

Miami, Atlanta, New York City

Everything I was doing at this time was all very new to me; Geechee Fred schooled me in every way. He would tell me what to wear, how to act, and what to do. I would do just what he told me to do. I was a very good student; I wanted to help him and please him.

I remember well the last night I worked in Miami. I was on my way to a bar downtown where some of the working girls picked up dates. The name of the club was Big Pop's. Back in those days, there weren't many girls walking the street, because there were some very nice clubs and bars that you could work out of.

On my way to Big Pop's, I met a man on the street who was drunk and wouldn't leave me alone. He kept following me, asking me to go out with him. I thought he was just drunk and kidding around. He said, "Baby, I've got some money." I thought he was joking, but when he pulled out this big ball of money, I stopped. "Okay, baby, what you want to do, honey?"

We got a cab and went to the rooming house; he had a bottle of liquor in his pocket that he kept pulling out and drinking from. This guy was a fool to be walking around with so much money on him and drunk. When we got to the room, this man lay on the bed and went out like a light. I could not wake him up. This was my first time rolling someone, just taking someone's money. So I was standing there, undecided as to what to do. Geechee Fred hadn't told me what to do if something like this came up. Man asleep, pocket full of money, what's a girl to do?

It took me a moment to realize this just might be a gift. I went through his pockets. There was a lot of money there. I didn't take all of his money because I felt bad about it. I left money for him so that when he woke up he could go where he needed to go. This was the first time I did anything like this. I got such a rush. And I was scared. I didn't want to try to catch a cab, because I was afraid the guy would wake up and call the cops and they would be looking for me.

I left the hotel and ran all the way back to Overtown, hiding behind buildings and houses all the way there. I ran all the way back to the club where we were living; when I got there, I showed all the money to Geechee Fred. He was shocked.

For the next few days he would not let me leave the club in case someone was looking for me. During those few days of staying in the club, all we did was pack up to leave town. He told me the day we were to leave that there was a change of plans—instead of going to New York, he needed to stop off in Atlanta to see a friend of his.

And so, I was finally on a Greyhound bus, one of the Greyhounds-to-heaven we watched in those cotton fields back in Mississippi—but I was heading to a life of hell.

In Atlanta, Geechee Fred's friend, Skinny Sam, was a barber who worked in a barbershop downtown on Peachtree Street. When Geechee Fred took me to Atlanta, he didn't tell me that Peachtree Street was a place where working girls hung out. The barbershop was a hangout for the girls' pimps, where they could keep an eye on their girls and the money.

We stayed in his friend's apartment for a few weeks. He took me out to a few nightclubs. There was an area in Atlanta called The Underground that wasn't far from Peachtree Street; this is where some of the pimps and their girls would go after work.

The Underground had all kinds of restaurants and nightclubs. This was my first time getting introduced to an after-hours club that would open after the regular clubs had closed and stay open until the early hours in the morning.

In some of the clubs, Geechee Fred would sing. He had a wonderful voice—something between Arthur Prysock and Billy Eckstine. One thing I knew for sure: he really loved singing, and for that reason I believed I had done the right thing. Life, for the moment, was good.

A few weeks after being at Skinny Sam's house, one day Geechee Fred told me to dress real nice with something sexy on because he wanted to take me down to the barbershop where Skinny Sam worked. It was very late in the evening and I wondered why the shop was open so late.

When we got to Peachtree Street, I saw a lot of girls standing on the street, and men came up to them. This looked like what I did in Miami, and this is when he told me what he wanted me to do. My heart sank. He said, "Baby, I am so sorry, we just do not have enough money to get to New York. You need to do this for just a few weeks, and I swear when we get to New York, you will be finished with this."

Once more he convinced me to do something I didn't want to do; I felt it was something that God did not approve of. I became very confused about the right and wrong of things. I had been abused so many times sexually, and had given it away quite a few times; I started not to feel bad because I was getting paid for it. I asked God to forgive me, and off I went.

As I was standing there, I noticed this little man going up to some of the girls and they all walked away from him. Then he came to me and asked if I wanted to go out; I said okay and told him how much. We went upstairs to the rooming house. I started to pull off my clothes, and this little man pulled off his pants. I had never seen a penis like that—it had to be a foot-and-a-half long, and the size of a beer can. I told him I was sorry but I wouldn't be able to do anything with him, that I just couldn't handle that. And the poor man started to cry.

It hit me—and it hit me hard—I just wanted to get out of that room, and out of Atlanta, and go back home to Mom. I put my clothes on and ran out of that room. I went into the barbershop where Geechee Fred was and I told him I couldn't do this, I wanted to go back to Miami, back to my family.

That is when I first saw the vicious side of this man. He grabbed me by the throat and took me out of the barbershop. It was very dark. He walked me to a bridge and told me that he would push me over the bridge and kill me right then and there if I tried to leave. He threatened that if I ran away he would hunt me down and kill me. He threatened that if I went back to Miami, he would kill my Mom and my sister. I begged and pleaded with him to please let me go back home, but he would not. This is when he started to control me with fear. That same night he beat me and raped me.

The following day he was back to being nice, and said he was sorry for treating me like that. He said he loved me and needed me.

We stayed in Atlanta for another three or four months, with me working making money, and him watching me from that barbershop.

My lifestyle changed. I had money, beautiful clothes to wear, and plenty of food. I started not to feel too bad because I still believed that once we got to New York, he would have enough money and we would just work in music. He still said he had money in the bank there, and that once we were there this would be finished.

All of this was a lie. All the lies he told me were to keep me from running away.

When we arrived in New York City, we came in on a Greyhound again. As we drove into the city, I was just blown away. I'd never seen anything like this. When we got to Grand Central Station, it was so big I thought it *was* the city! In this place, there were so many people and they all were moving so fast, it was like a school of fish rushing past. My life went from zero to 100 the minute I stepped off the bus into Grand Central Station. I was amazed at the tall buildings and how people were moving—if you didn't get out of the way, they would run over you, or you would get carried along with the crowd.

Where I came from, people would see each other on the street and speak. I learned quickly that you just don't do that in the city. I would walk down the street speaking to people and they would look at me like was a damn fool.

Another thing I saw in the city that I didn't see in Miami: people were knocked out or sleeping in the street, and people would just walk over them. One day I watched a man slumped over; he was bent over and his body kept getting closer and closer to the ground, but he never fell down. I kept thinking someone should help him. I went to help him and was shocked when he didn't want my help; he wanted me to leave him alone after asking if I had a dollar. I found out later what was going on: these people were on drugs, and most of them were shooting up heroin.

We rented an efficiency in one of the hotels on Broadway called The Whitehall. Something else about New York that Miami didn't have: most of the hotels had a buzzer that would buzz you in and out. There were many things I had to get used to in New York.

We had a very cozy efficiency with a little kitchen overlooking Broadway. This apartment building was on Broadway between 70th and 71st Street. Everything we needed was within a couple of blocks—a grocery store, bars, restaurants, all kinds of shops; everything was right downstairs, and I was fascinated by the place. So we got settled down in the apartment at The Whitehall and I was very happy to be there. I knew I could breathe easy because we were here in New York, now this guy can get his money, we can really get the music going, everything is going be all right.

That was a big joke in my head—I was hoping that this was real. I really believed him.

Please remember that when I met Geechee Fred I was around 18 years old; he was 20 years older; he could've been my Daddy. He was a great deceiver and a manipulator. He played me and he played me well. For the next 15 years I was to continue being a pawn in his hand, and a personal punching bag. He took complete control of me, and I let him.

Geechee Fred manipulated me in every way—not only my body and mind, but also spiritually. He was a strong believer in Allah and had been a follow of Mohammed since the late '50s and early '60s. He'd done some time in prison, about seven years, and that is when he was introduced to Islam. When he came out of prison, he never went to any of the temples, and never took me to one. He just kept his own personal beliefs about Allah and he taught those beliefs to me. He felt that everything he did was in the name of Allah, and the things he had me do was me being a good woman and a good servant to Allah.

Later on, after my breakup with Geechee Fred, I went to a temple to be a part of Islam, and I found out how caring they are to women. The Muslims here in the United States have a great respect for their women. This guy had his own personal cult going on with me and I was his only member.

At some point in life you are totally responsible for yourself and all the things you do. You can't keep blaming your Mom or your Dad or the slave master, it is you. We all have a consciousness and a conscience, and most of the men that were dealing with me were very vicious. Those guys, when I was young, they were young too, and maybe they didn't know how wrong their behavior toward me and other women was.

But Geechee Fred was an older man, just rotten to the core; very simply, he hated women. If he could have forgiven his mother, I might have had a chance, but no, he used that to hurt others. And it wasn't only women he hated. He had two sons, and he didn't like them or the women who had them, either.

Before I got a forgiven and forgiving heart, I used to blame God as if God just let these things happen to me. God had nothing to do with what went on in my life; I was totally responsible for it. It was a while before I got this.

New York City

Coming to New York put me 1,200 miles from my family and friends. I was isolated and in Geechee Fred's complete control. He told me that it would be different in New York, because we would work on music, do some shows, and make money that way, not by me selling my body.

From our sixth-floor apartment, I could look out the window and see Broadway and people move like ants up and down the street. I fell in love with New York. There was something about the rhythm, the smell, the people—I became more alive, and I'd never felt so good.

One day, Geechee Fred said he was going to take me to Harlem where a lot of musicians live. He wanted to introduce me to his piano player, so he could start working with me and training my voice. We went to a brownstone building that had about five floors to it. Every floor had some type of training going on. One floor was for people training in dancing, another floor for people taking piano or guitar lessons—this was a very busy place.

When I met Fred's piano player, I was surprised at how small he was—he was a tiny little man and they called him Mr. Smell. But when he got on that piano and started to play, he became a giant—the man could play his butt off. He had me sing something for him, and he told Geechee Fred that I had a beautiful voice, but I needed a lot of work. He said that he would take me under his wing and teach me. Finally I was going to get the training I needed to become a great singer, and I was willing to pay whatever price.

Well, this was another thing that didn't work out. I went to see Mr. Smell three times, and each time Geechee Fred was there and wouldn't let me work with the man. Next thing I heard, Mr. Smell had passed away. That was yet another failure for me.

Looking back, all Geechee Fred was doing in Miami and in Atlanta was grooming me for New York.

After a few weeks, he left the hotel one day and was gone for a few hours. When he came back, he had that sad look on his face, the same look he had back at the Overtown club when he told me the money he thought he had was gone and he was broke. That night, he said that somehow or another we had to pay the rent for this apartment or get kicked out.

L ooking for a trick, I didn't need to go far, because there were guys in the hotel who wanted to have a date with me, and I picked up a few regulars. There were girls working all up and down Broadway and some girls working in the bars.

One night I made a very bad mistake, and I'm lucky I didn't lose my life.

While I was walking down Broadway, a man pulled up to me in a car and asked for a date. I said okay and I got into his car to go to the hotel. I was so country I still trusted in people. I got into his car and told him the way to the hotel. This man took off going down the wrong street. I said, "You're not going the right way to the hotel," but he wouldn't say anything—he just kept driving. I said to him, "Would you please just stop and let me out," but still he was silent and kept driving.

Then I went to reach for the door handle and there was no damn door handle. I couldn't open the door to get out of the car. My God, this man is going to kill me!

He drove to the Hudson Parkway, got into traffic, and drove fast for about three or four miles down the road. He stopped and pulled the car off the road. I found out later that this place was next to Riverside Park.

He had something in his hand and told me to get out. I got out of the car and he told me to walk into the bushes. When I turned around, I saw that he had a gun. This is when he told me to take off all my clothes. I went into a state of shock and did what he told me to do. This man was getting ready to blow my head off when he heard something, grabbed all my clothes and my purse, and got into his car and drove off.

I was left on the side of the road completely naked. I got up and tried to flag a car down, but no one would stop. When no one would stop, I started walking. Then I saw long stairs that led over to the park. I walked up and over the stairs, and pulled some branches off the trees to cover myself. I walked up to this couple, and I'm sure I shocked the hell out of them. I was crying and asked them to help me—I gave them the phone number for Geechee Fred. They called him and waited around for a while for him to show up. Wherever you are, whoever you are, thank you.

When Geechee Fred got there, the couple showed him where I was and left. I never learned their names. I was lying there in the bushes with no clothes on—he was mad at *me* and threw my clothes at me, calling me all kinds of names. A few days later, he beat me. He hated me for what happened. The shame I felt is is still with me today; he never let me live that down.

After that, I knew without question that this man hated me—still I was too afraid to leave. I just did not have the courage to go out on my own. In my mind I was trapped with no way out. Back in those days you didn't have the help that abused women have today. Nowadays they have help for every abuse for women, children, old people, even pets. In my own mind, I just kept making adjustments to survive. Your mind can be your best friend or your worst enemy.

I started working the streets, mostly on the West Side. I made myself like what I was doing. I would pretend I was someone else—my name for that new person was Juice Sweet. I was out there with all the other working girls, working both the bars and the streets.

Once I met a girl I called Fast Talking Fanny. Everything she would do was fast—she would walk fast, talk fast, and turn a trick fast.

One night her fast life came to an end. She and a girl she worked with all the time tried to pull a fast one on a date. I found out later that she and the other girl tried to take the man's money. The date caught her and killed her in the elevator, and the other girl was able to get away. This guy had just gotten out of a mental institution.

After that night, I was a lot more fearful, but was still going out trying to work with the fear that maybe this one might be a killer. It was very stressful.

One night I had a date with a black man. Usually I wouldn't go out with a black man, because most of time they want to rape you or rob you. It was a slow night and something told me not to go with this guy, but he seemed to be nice. We went to the hotel, which was right around the corner, and he gave the money to the desk clerk for the room. We got inside and closed the door. I had my back turned for a moment—I turned around and the guy had a knife in his hand. He told me to give him my money. I said I didn't have any. He told me to take my clothes off. I said, "Brother, please don't do this, we black people don't have the money, go to the white man and rob him." Well, the man stabbed me in my stomach and ran out the door.

I went home. I lived right up the street. I told Geechee Fred what had happened, but I didn't tell him it was a black man—if I had, he would beat the hell out of me. Most of us girls knew that the brothers didn't want to pay, they would just take what they wanted. I never did go to the hospital. We did what we had to do. It wasn't a deep wound. I think the brother wasn't trying to hurt me badly; he did that to give him some time to get away.

After that, I started to work the bars more, and started working sometimes as a call girl for $100 a date. Life felt good and I had the best of everything: nice clothes, food, a nice place to stay, and the devil in my arms every night after work. Geechee Fred would stay high all the time—and the higher he got, the freakier he became. It was nothing for Geechee Fred to down a fifth of liquor a day, a half gram of cocaine, and top it off with some marijuana. I became his personal slave. His every wish was my command. He was one of my biggest tricks—only thing was, I gave him all the pleasures and all the money.

We moved farther up the West Side off of Amsterdam Avenue, into a one-bedroom apartment in a four-story brownstone. I will never forget that apartment building, because across the street from where we lived, one of the working girls and her pimp killed a cop. The pimp's name was Carlo; her name was Redhead Sally from South Carolina. Carlo was so jealous of Redhead Sally that when she had a date he would stand outside the door until she was finished. It was kind of a safety net for her, but crazy as hell—if he loved her that much, why would he have her in such a business?

One day I came out of the apartment to go to the store, and cops were everywhere. I saw them putting handcuffs on Carlo and

Redhead Sally and put them into a squad car. Later on that night, I found out that they had killed a cop, chopped him up, and put him in a garbage bag.

What helped keep me from going crazy with all that was going on around me was thinking about the music.

Sheba in McGowan's Bar on Broadway

New York
and the music

Finally! Finally we began doing something with the music. I was very happy because it looked like at last Geechee Fred was keeping his word on this part. Getting involved with the music, I started to feel not so bad about what I was doing to get the money—we started using some of the money towards the music. I was two people: Sweet Juice at night, Lady M in the day time.

We started putting on shows—we would rent a ballroom and sell tickets. Back then New York had very nice ballrooms in some of the older hotels. It turned out that Geechee Fred did know plenty of people in the music business; it was no problem for him to get a band together, horns and all. We would have singers, dancers, and always a comedian; each person who was in the show would sell tickets. Most of the time, before the night of the show, all tickets were sold out, and this is how the other entertainers got paid. What would piss me off with Greeche Fred is that he would drinking the whole night and by the end of the show he would have a fight with someone. After a few of the shows, the police came and took him to jail.

Another thing is he still would not let me sing by myself. I would sing with him. He called us The Swingers.

I was living a double life—a call girl by night, and a high-class lady and singer by day. Most of the people in the entertainment business didn't know.

We worked some of the best jazz clubs in New York, and I met some great people. I'll never forget the night I met Arthur Prysock in Harlem in a club called Mr. B's. It was such a pleasure to meet him! I have always loved his voice; he was like a big giant standing over me. I got to meet Carmen McRae, Redd Foxx,

Flip Wilson, and many others. I got very close to meeting James Brown.

Geechee Fred sometimes would work doing hair up in Harlem. Just like everything he did, it was half-assed; he was a half-ass at hairstyles. In those days, many entertainers wore processed hair and this shop was one of the places they would come to.

One day I went to meet Geechee Fred at the shop, and that's when I found out I had just missed James Brown. Geechee Fred looks so much like James Brown that some people thought he *was* James Brown; he was about the same height and size, and both wore the same type of processes. When I got there, people were still coming into the shop, speaking to Geechee Fred, thinking he was James Brown.

We put on shows at some of the top hotels of the time: the Riverside Hotel, the Manhattan Hotel (this was when this hotel was farther up Broadway; it had another name but I can't think of it), the Beacon Hotel, to name a few. One club was called Under the Stairs, and another one next to it was called Jimmy Ryan; both places were great supper clubs. Under the Stairs was a very elegant club, with white linen tablecloths, and the waiters were dressed in black and white tails. Jimmy Ryan was more like a dance club; people did a lot of drinking. I loved singing in these places because it gave me a chance to wear beautiful gowns and to forget my night (after-hours) job.

We got a chance to play at the Village Gate. That's where I met Al Hibbler. He was blind but his blindness didn't stop him from being a great pianist and singer. He had a big hit out of his recording of "Unchained Melody."

Geechee Fred introduced

The Village Gate.
Courtesy Getty Archives

me to some of the greatest musicians on the planet; at the time I didn't know how great those people were. When I started writing this book, I started looking them up on the Internet—the ones I could find, I was totally surprised. Looking back, I am so proud of myself that with the money I was making we could afford the best musicians in town. Geechee Fred knew these guys, but my hard-earned money kept them there.

Things started changing for me as a working girl. I started meeting dates that had plenty of money and were very good to me. I remember the night I met the Minister—I was standing on Broadway in the winter and it was very cold. This man came up to me—he had on an overcoat, a big scarf wrapped around his neck, and a hat pulled down so low you could hardly see his eyes. He asked me if I wanted a date, we talked, I said what it was, and he said okay.

Once we were in our room, he told me he wanted some cocaine. He gave me the money to go get it, and when I got back, he wanted me to take off my clothes, leave my panties and bra on, and feed him the coke. I would put the coke on my fingernail and he would snort it. He just played with himself, never reaching a climax, just playing with himself. I walked off that night with $1,000 for a few hours.

After that, he kept coming back every two or three weeks. Each time he would come, he wanted more and more cocaine and added heroin. To make it more fun for him, I added more girls and we all would dress in sexy lingerie for him. He gave me money to make sure that I would buy some sexy lingerie for the girls and me.

I kept wondering who this man was, and one night I got my answer when the television was signing off. In those days, every night a minister, rabbi, or priest would do a prayer before the television station signed off for the night. So this man, it turned out, was a big-time minister. I was shocked.

We did our first recording in 1978 with a big band including some well-known musicians in the jazz world. George Kelly (1915-1998, an original member of the Savoy Sultans) was a tenor saxophone player who arranged all our music; he was known all over the world, and he was in charge of getting the band together. Well-known pianist Sonny Donaldson played with us. We had Matthew Gee on trombone, Tiny Grimes on guitar, Panama Francis on drums, Howard McGhee (one of the first bebop jazz trumpeters) on trumpet, and Morris on bass (I don't remember his last name). In the brass section, most of the guys could play more than one horn.

Those were the guys we used on our recording and some of the dates we played. Most of them had come to the end of their heyday, and drugs and alcohol had beaten some of them down. One thing was bad about a lot of those jazz musicians: their drug of choice was shooting up heroin and drinking, and a lot of them died from one or both.

I have some of the recordings we did in the studio—a 45 RPM and some tapes that I've made .mp3s of in order to preserve them. When I listen to these recordings, they still blow me away. Those musicians were so incredibly talented.

With what I know now, if I had a band like that behind me today, I could do some great things. It was a blessing to be around such gifted musicians and to have them back up my voice; the sound is amazing. I should have listened to them when they said I should go solo.

On that first 45, we recorded Geechee Fred's song, "That's Jazz." I wrote "Ain't It Grand." We did them as a duo. On another recording, I wrote two of the two songs and did them alone: "I Love You" and "Don't Say Goodbye." Geechee Fred wrote "Born to Love You" and "Lost Love" and recorded them alone. Together, we wrote our theme song called "The Swingers," which was also the name of our group. We both liked writing songs; some of the songs I wrote while I was with him I recorded years later after leaving him.

My first time going into the studio, I was very excited about it. I was making good money, so we could afford the studio and all the musicians. However, I didn't like the fact that every time we would have a show, practice, or go into the studio, a lot of drugs and liquor were always around. Geechee Fred didn't need to be drinking—first thing he would do was start a fight with somebody. We had booked several hours at the studio to do the recording of six songs, and this was a big band.

Things were going well when about four hours into our recording session someone pissed him off. The manager of the studio called it a day and told everyone there would be no more drinking in his studio while recording. Everyone came back the following day; with no drinking, we got the musicians recorded, and everything went well. The following days we went in and recorded some of the vocals with George Kelly, Geechee Fred, and myself, and that went well too.

The people at the studio were very happy with my voice and wanted to talk to me about doing some more recordings for them. However, Geechee Fred told them they had to talk to him, because I was his woman and wouldn't be recording for anyone else.

After recording those songs, we never did go back into the studio. As a matter of fact, most of the shows and club dates stopped. I believe he became jealous of my voice, because after each show we did, people would always come over to me, praising my voice. I would look over to where he was, and see the look on his face. He hated that they weren't praising him. I would try to downplay myself and tell them that it was because of him that I sang the way I did.

Thus, it seemed that everything stopped musically for me. Rather than Geechee Fred backing me up and saying the people really like my voice, let me get behind you and help you be a great singer, he became jealous and made us stop everything. I'm not going to beat up on myself because I let him do that. I still was not strong enough to go by myself.

During all this time, I was still seeing the Minister. He was a great date for me and I stayed with him for years. There were times I started writing my own checks. I saw him once a month, and some nights I walked away with $20,000. I would tell him I paid $500 for a bag of coke—it would only be $25, but sometimes it would be up to about 25 bags. The same thing with the heroin. I would get cash from him, and when he ran out of cash, he would give me a check. I would never deposit his check; he would meet me the following day with cash and I would give him the check back. Often, he wanted parties with several girls. He only wanted black girls. Each beautiful girl would take turns feeding him the cocaine—the rest of the girls would be in the other room having their own party. When I had these parties, I made sure there was plenty of cocaine and drinks for everyone.

Every year, the Minister would go out of the country for two or three months, and when he got back he was always more than ready to get it on.

Among the nights I'll never forget is this one: after one of his trips, he called me from the airport and said he wanted to see me. He told me he had a briefcase with him and he wouldn't have time to stop by his house. I said okay, bring it, it will be all right, and he did—but I didn't know it was full of money. I rented the suite, called the girls, and got some stuff for him. I spent about three hours with him and the girls getting high and me drinking, when he said he wanted to go someplace and party more.

A club had just opened up called Plato's Retreat. People walked around naked; it was a big room with a pad on the floor with people having sex all over the place. We got a cab and went to this place and he carried the briefcase with him. By this time I knew he had money in it, and I was hoping the girls wouldn't take his money. There were about six of us in the cab including him. When we got there, one of the girls reached to help him out of the car and that damn briefcase flew open. All of that money fell out onto the ground. You want to talk about honor among thieves, those girls picked up every bill and put it back into that briefcase. Thank you, girls.

Things got so bold with him and me, a few times when his money ran out I would call my personal cab driver to pick me up and take me to his house for him to get more money. I would sit

82

in the cab down the street waiting on him. Sometimes it took 20 minutes or more. This cab driver I could call when I needed him; of course I was very kind and gracious to him. If I needed him to pick up any of the other girls, he would.

Well, the Minister heard about this new thing called freebasing. At the time, freebasing was where you would mix cocaine and heroin, and smoke it thought a pipe. One of the girls had a trick who had a heart attack while smoking that pipe, and some of the girls were getting hooked on it—they stopped caring for themselves and looked very strange. All they wanted was to hit the pipe. Every dime they made went to the pipe, and a lot of them destroyed themselves.

I got it for him along with the pipe, and cooked it up for him a few times. The last date I had with him I will never forget. He could have died, and I would have gone to jail. That night, the Minister wanted me and one other girl. Her name was Blackberry; her skin was very dark, and she was a sweet girl who didn't do drugs. We all met at the hotel. I had the stuff, we went to the room, I was drinking, and he was smoking and enjoying himself.

He took a big puff of that pipe and just held his breath. I looked at him and I said to Blackberry, "He isn't letting air out!" The damn man was not breathing and was turning colors. I said, *hell* no. We pulled him out of the bed and dragged him over to the bathtub. Somehow or another, we got him into the tub. We ran cold water on him and put ice in the tub all around him. Then I heard this big sigh. He came back, thank God. It was over for us—I did not want to have any part of someone getting killed.

Dates

In between seeing the Minister, I had other dates, and a few were good to me. One who was very kind to me was Sweet John, a little white man about five-feet-four. Sweet John became a good friend and I stayed with him for years, even after I got out of the business. After I broke up with Geechee Fred and moved back to Florida, Sweet John stood by me. When I went back to school and got my cosmetology license, Sweet John came to visit me in Florida and gave me $10,000 to get started with my own hair shop. He met my family, and every year on Mother's Day he would send my Mom flowers. Everyone in my family loved him.

Sweet John was a big drinker. He loved Heineken—he drank beer every waking moment. He worked as a maintenance man at one of the big hotels in Manhattan where he had a two-bedroom apartment. I spent many weekends in that apartment. I would meet him at a neighborhood bar called Toney's, where the locals would hang out. Some working girls who lived in the neighborhood would pick up dates there; if you were nice and carried yourself well you could work out of this bar.

The night I met Sweet John, he was sitting at the bar hanging on to that bottle of Heineken. I took the seat next to him and introduced myself, and he said, "Can I buy you a drink?" After a few drinks I told him what I did. He said he knew, and that he had been watching me and he liked me.

From that night on we were stuck to each other; he wouldn't go out with any other girl. I would meet Sweet John after he got off work. We would sit at the bar and drink until the bar closed; I knew he would give me the money I needed for the whole night. We would leave the bar, go to his apartment, freak out all night, drink, and just enjoy each other's company. We really fell for each other. It felt so good being around him; only thing was, Geechee Fred would always remind me that he was just a trick.

No matter what he said, I didn't feel that way about my Sweet John. I would have run away with him, but he was married. He had a wife in Brooklyn that he would go out to see once a week to take care of things around the house. Besides, if I were to leave and let Sweet John set me up and take care of me, I was deathly afraid that Geechee Fred would find and kill both of us. God only knew what Geechee Fred was doing when I went to work. He was off the chain. I spent weekends with Sweet John, and on Monday morning I would go home.

One weekend, I had left my makeup at home, so I dropped by the house to pick it up. Geechie Fred didn't hear me come in. I heard some sounds coming from the bedroom—I slowly opened the door, and he was pumping some young boy. I closed the door and got the hell out of there; at this point I was terribly afraid of him and stayed away. I really didn't care what he did as long as he stayed off my case.

Sweet John was so good to me he would let me use his credit card to buy all kinds of things. I would buy clothes, shoes, appliances, whatever, and he was good with the money; he just wanted to help me. I even got to know his children, who were all grown. He had one daughter who hated my guts and two sons. They lived in Brooklyn—one son lived with his mother and the others had their own places. Sometimes they came to Manhattan to visit with their father and hang out in the bar. His daughter didn't want me messing with her father. She was friends with the owner of the bar, and many times she would say things to try and get me kicked out of the bar.

One night I came into the bar. She was with a couple of friends and her Dad was there, too. She got up in my face telling me to leave her Dad alone. I told her, you tell your Dad to leave me alone. I said to her, if you do not get out of my face, I'm going to slap the hell out of you. She didn't. I did. No one moved, and her father looked the other way.

Besides Heineken and me, Sweet John loved his boat and was very proud of it. We went out on it a few times to go fishing, he and a few of his friends—we all had a good time.

One time I invited a girlfriend of mine to go out with us. We went out, drinking and swimming, no fishing. Things were going well, but I saw the clouds starting to get dark. The wind picked up and the weather turned bad quickly. We all had being drinking a lot, and Sweet John wasn't thinking clearly. He started to drive the boat in the wrong direction. To get us back to land, we had to go west, but he was going east, out into the open ocean. This was another one of those times when I feared for my life. I begged John to look at the compass. Finally he did look down and turned that boat around and got us out of there, but I never did go back out there again.

For years I stayed in contact with him. When he passed away, one of his sons contacted me and told me that his father had died. Sweet John was gone, and I knew that it was his wish for me to know of his passing. Sweet John, you will always be a part of my heart, thank you.

If I wasn't so full of fear of Geechee Fred, I would have gotten away from him. People would ask, why not leave? But fear is very powerful.

Before I had met Geechee Fred, I had several depressions and I'd had some severe panic attacks. When I met Geechee Fred, for some reason the panic attacks went away and stayed away for a few years. Then they slowly started to come back, but he became a safe person for me because when I would have one and go to him they went away. I never told him what was going on with me because I thought I was losing my mind.

Panic attacks can happen at any time, even when you're asleep. People having a panic attack might feel that they are having a heart attack, going crazy, or even dying. You can imagine the physical symptoms that came along with this including having trouble breathing and being out of control. Back in those days they didn't have the help that they have now for panic attacks. Don't be like me—I kept it in and wouldn't tell anyone. I am sure if I had said something back then they would have called me crazy and locked me up.

During that life, I met some very strange people—guys wanting to be tied up, beat up, pissed on. You name it, it was there. One of the strangest things was the guy who came to me wanting someone to cut his penis off. I said, "You've got to be kidding." I told another girl because I damn sure was not going to do that. I don't know what happened and didn't want to know.

Things started to change in the business in New York in the 1980s. AIDS emerged, and freebasing became a thing. AIDS showed up big-time in the early '80s. People became afraid. Until then, a true working girl had been very safe—she would always use condoms and look a date over to see if there any visible signs of venereal disease like sores.

But AIDS didn't work like that. You couldn't see it. And it was a death sentence. This was not only working girls, this was the whole population. Everyone was vulnerable to this.

I'd seen freebasing with the Minister, but crack started to be a thing. In the Minister's day, they mixed cocaine with heroin and smoked it, but crack was synthetic cocaine and they smoked that.

Smoking that pipe, many people lost everything. I'm not talking about just people in the ghetto, this stuff went to the top and got your doctors, lawyers, all kinds of businesspeople. White people, black people, red people, yellow people, you name it, people were hooked.

One of the saddest things was to see some of the girls I used to work with. These were beautiful girls from all over the United States—Texas, Washington, you name it, they all came to New York. To see some of those ladies in the finest clothes, wearing the best jewelry, and having the best of everything—to see those girls go down to nothing, walking the streets, not asking for a date, but begging for a handout—it was devastating.

The same thing was going on with their pimps—once in a while you'd see one of the pimps dressed up in a miniskirt and heels. All I can say about that is, payback is a bitch.

This was when we closed up shop, packed up, and moved back to Florida. Geechee Fred became full of fear—not of what I was doing, but of his own lifestyle. I had gotten to the point where I didn't want him touching me.

Coming back to Florida, some major things were going to happen to help me escape the clutches of this devil Geechee Fred. During the time that I was with him, I didn't get into using heavy drugs. He tried to get me on drugs, because it would have kept the money coming to support our habit. But that experience in my past—smoking marijuana that someone had put something into—that incident saved my life.

Geechee Fred, Florida, and crack

Geechee Fred was born in Gretna, Florida, a town about 20 miles away from Tallahassee. While I was with him, his father was living there. It is a very small town, and most of the work there is farm work—picking tomatoes, beans, squash, just like it was back in Homestead, Florida when I was a child.

By the time we returned to Florida, Geechee Fred's father was 75 years old. Even at that age he was still growing all kinds of vegetables and selling them—greens of all kinds, and string beans, and more. He did very well at growing and selling his vegetables.

During our stay in New York, we would send money to him to save because Geechee Fred hoped someday to move back to his home town. I'd seen the hate he had for his mother, but when we moved down to Gretna, I saw the hatred he had for his Dad too.

When we got there, we found out that his Dad had a girlfriend and had spent some of the money on her. This pissed Geeche Fred off. His father said he would pay the money back—and later on, he decided to put his home in Geechee Fred's name. That was a bad mistake. After Geechee Fred's name was on the deed, he decided to take out a loan on the house. Somehow or another, he had my name on the loan too. When the money came clear for the loan on the house, I knew that if this man got his hands on this money he was going to blow it all, and there were things that needed to be fixed in the house.

Fortunately for me, Geechee Fred did something and went to jail. I was able to use the money to fix up the house. It was all planned out before we got the money what things we were going to do in the house. I was very happy not having him around, and I got the job done.

While Geechee Fred was gone, I had some very nice conversations with his father. He told me that Geechee Fred's mother, Geechee Cora, was a mean and hateful woman, and he became afraid of her. Once he found a way to get away from her, he left and didn't look back. If he went back or she could find him, he was sure she would hurt or kill him. He said she had a bad reputation of using a razor on people—or, worse, potash. Back in the day, people were bad about using potash. They would throw it on a person and it would eat away their skin. He said this is where Geechee Fred got all of that hate from—his mother—and he told me that I needed to get away from him.

Once we went to visit his mother, Geechee Cora, and this is when I thought he was going to beat her up. He was all in her face, talking bad about the things she had done to him when he was a child. He would say to her about how she would take things from him and give them to his brother because she said he was going to be a preacher one day. She was crying, begging him to stop. He wouldn't—he picked her up, and I screamed for him to please put her down, don't hurt her. I thought he was going to slam dunk his own mother to the ground. Thank God, he didn't, he just picked her up and put her down. Geechee Cora had only two boys and she did pick over the two. For some reason she hated Geechee Fred; I guess he was too much like her. When she passed away, he didn't go to her funeral; he was glad she was gone.

Geechee Fred had two sons from one lady, and one daughter from another. He hated them all, and the women who had them. He would talk about his sons and never would say anything about his daughter; I guess that was how much he hated women. When we lived in New York, occasionally we came back to Florida to visit his children and bring things to them. He would give the boys some of the money that I made, but he would treat them like hell the way he would talk down to them. The boys' mother he would call a fat pig and talk down to her about the way she had raised the boys, yet he wasn't there to help her—he disappeared out of their lives when they were babies.

When Geechee Fred got out of jail, he was pissed at me and wanted some of the money. I gave him a few dollars so he could have some crack for a few days. After the money was gone, he started stealing things out of the house, selling them for drugs. All of the jewelry I had, and whatever was in the house that had some value, he stole and took them to the pawn shop or sold them to someone.

Things started changing with him. He was going downhill fast, with all the drinking and drugs he used. In New York, he still carried himself well, but when we got down to a little town like Gretna he decided to get on crack. He told me he was going to get on crack to lose weight. This man started leaving home and would be gone for days wearing the same clothes—this was a a man who would change clothes two to three times a day in New York. It got so bad with him he would bring his crack home and take it to his room and smoke that pipe. I would disappear—I didn't want him touching me. He had his room and I had mine. He would go in there and smoke and masturbate.

Even with all the liquor and drugs he was using, Geechee Fred didn't want me to drink. So I would wait until he passed out, and then I would jump into the car, go into town, and get some beer. I learned to time it just right. We were in the country, about ten miles out of town. My round trip would take about 25 minutes and he would be out for a few hours. I would enjoy my beer, and if he had some liquor left I would have some of that too, and put water back in the bottle. When he would wake up to see me all happy running around the house, he would ask me what was wrong with me. I wouldn't say anything. I never overdid it, just drank enough to give me a buzz where he couldn't tell.

Crack was bad in this little town. It was everywhere. Geechee Fred had no problem finding people who sold it and smoked it. He started hanging with some very strange people and would be gone from home for days.

It got to the point where we had no money and had to go to work in the fields picking tomatoes and beans. My mind went all the way back to Mississippi when I was a child in the cotton fields and in south Florida picking tomatoes and beans. That gave me strength to do what I had to do. I worked those fields and made the money I needed. Geechee Fred had a hard time because he had never done this type of work before. All he knew was how to use others by being a half-assed pimp. Whatever money I made, I kept it to buy food for the house and pay bills. Whatever money he made, he could do whatever he wanted to do with it.

I no longer gave him any of the money I made, and it was much more then he made. After leaving New York and having some time to think in Florida, I had made up my mind I was through with that. It was amazing that I had no problem going back to work in those fields; this taught me that I was a survivor. Geechee Fred went through hell working in those fields, but he had to do it if he wanted some crack. I was not giving up any more of my money.

Later, we both went to work in the tomato plant, grading tomatoes, picking out the bad tomatoes. I was very contented with what I was doing. I started canning tomatoes and freezing beans and okra. A lady who lived down the street from us knew how to make quilts, and she showed me how. This took me back to my grandmother and her friends on the porch making quilts. They would have us kids pick the seeds out of the cotton that was going to go inside of the quilts. I loved every moment of being with her, and this took my mind off that fool.

I was not sad at all about not having the money I had in New York; I was at peace. Most of the time Geechee Fred wasn't around. This gave me time to grow and learn more about myself.

Geechee Fred shoots me

Geechee Fred and I worked for several months in the tomato plant. He was still doing his thing, going to work some days and staying out all night doing his crack.

One day he came to me and said he wanted to go to Miami and pick up some crack to bring back to Gretna and sell. In this little town the crack was running out, so he came up with the idea of driving down to Miami to pick up more. Miami was big and had plenty of crack everywhere.

He said he was going to call his oldest son to come from Jacksonville to do some of the driving, and he wanted me go and help. I saw the shape he was in, and it was bad. For days the man had been going stone crazy. I knew that if I got on the road with that fool somebody would die.

He did call his son. Geechee Fred had a bad habit—when other men were around, he would show them how he thought a woman should be treated, and the way he would talk to me was very abusive. The day we were to leave, Geechee Fred had tried to force me to go, but then he started going off on me for no reason. That is when I stood my ground and told him I wouldn't go.

I was so happy to stay home. The days he was gone were good days. His father was there in the house, so I wasn't alone. At this point, most of the time his father would stay in his room with his door locked; sometimes he would go stay with his girlfriend for days. He was afraid of his son and wasn't too sure what he might do to him. While Geechee Fred was gone, his Dad had another talk with me and said I should leave him because he was no good. I said to him, "I hate your son, mostly I'm staying because I don't want to see him hurt you."

For a few days I didn't hear from Geechee Fred. I was thinking about calling the State Police so they could catch him on the highway on his way home and put him into jail. A few days went by and I didn't hear anything from Geechee Fred.

On the fourth day, I got a call from his son's mother— she told me that his father hit him and threw him out of the car somewhere along the highway. She had to send money for him to catch a Greyhound bus and come home. If I had gone, he would have done the same thing to me or worse. Another couple of days passed and he still didn't call me. I was hoping that he was in jail or dead.

On day six, I got a call from him saying that the car had broken down somewhere along I-75 and he needed me to come get him and the car. I went to U-Haul to rent a car trailer so we could pull the car back to Gretna. The person who rented me the trailer showed me what to do to make sure that the trailer was properly hitched to the car. Geechee Fred was in a little place called Cooperstown, about 20 miles north of Lake City.

When I pulled up, the first thing he said to me was that he was going to beat my ass when we get home, because if I had gone this wouldn't have happened.

I told him what the man at U-Haul had told me about how to hook up the car and trailer. He wouldn't listen and told me to shut up. I saw that he was high—he looked like a wild man and smelled like a skunk that had been dead for a week. I told him to let me drive, but he refused.

When we get back onto I-75, he got into the fast lane. When he did that, I told him he needed to be in the slow lane and he needed to slow down. But Geechee Fred stayed in the fast lane and wouldn't move over. He said, "These people need to watch out for me," and the moment he said that something happened— something came loose on the trailer. We started fish-tailing and went off the road, into the woods.

When the car came to a stop, this fool got out and started blaming me and yelling, with his hand in his pocket where he kept his gun. He was telling me that if I had gone with him, none of this stuff would have happened. It was night and very dark. I flipped out and started walking off into the woods. I said, if you're going to shoot me, do it now—I'm walking off into these woods, you wouldn't have to worry about hiding the body, something would eat my ass up. He must've thought about it, that he would be out there by himself and would have no one to help him. He told me, "Girl, get your butt back here," and that's when I snapped out of it and said, "We are in trouble and somehow or another we need to get home."

By this time it was in the mid-'80s and cell phones were rare. Someone must have gone to the next exit and called the police, because an officer did show up. He saw that no one was hurt and no one was at fault, but he told us the car wasn't drivable because the right front tire had blown and was down to the rim. Geechee Fred told the policeman that we had a spare and we would put that on, and the policeman said okay and left. However, when we looked in the back of the car, there was no spare tire—that fool must've sold it for some crack and forgot. We left the broken-down car on the trailer there, and Geechee Fred got into the car with the flat tire and drove it on the side of the road for those ten miles. We found a place that fixed the tire and rim with money I had.

When we got home, he told me he was going to beat my ass because I didn't do my womanly duties; this is that old pimp talk that has poisoned so many young girls' minds. I begged and pleaded with him to just let me get some rest because it was so late. He wouldn't stop talking. I stood there listening to everything he had to say, but I knew that soon he would give up and go smoke. Finally he went into his room to get off, and just left me alone, thank God.

The next day he called on some of the boys around town to help him go pick up the car and trailer. Most likely they were a bunch of guys he'd promised some crack to.

Unbelievably, later I got a call saying they were about 60 miles from Gretna and had ran out of gas. Off I went to save those fools with two gallons of gas, just enough to get them all back to Gretna. I had them follow me back so I could keep an eye on them in case something else happened. Looking back on all this, many times I'd been ready to leave this guy, but I didn't. It was mostly because of the fear and the way I let him program my mind.

When I got home, it was late. Geechee Fred went to take the guys home and give them whatever he was going to. All I wanted to do was just get away from him, go into my room and not come out. He came home an hour or so later—I heard him go into his room. I was beginning to feel good—maybe he would leave me alone. Well, 15 minutes later, I heard him call me, and he said, I told you I was going to beat your ass. I said we're all safe, everything is all right, please just leave me alone.

I went into the bathroom, but he followed me in and said he was going to kill me. I broke away from him and ran to the kitchen. I was looking for something to defend myself with. I was tired of the beatings and the threats; I felt he really was going to try to kill me this time. When I got to the kitchen, I was looking for a knife, when I heard this loud noise and the shattering of something. I turned around and he was standing there with the gun in his hand. I looked down, and glass was all around my feet and my left thigh was bleeding. At that point time I just went after him with the knife in my hand. The man could have kept shooting me, I didn't care. I ran at him with the knife in my hand—he dropped the gun and took the knife away from me.

I calmed down and realized that I had to go to the hospital. We had a fifth of liquor on the dining room table, and I picked it up and started drinking it. He took me to the hospital, but he wouldn't go all the way. He dropped me off on a side road. He was afraid that if he went in, they would arrest him.

After the doctors treated the wound, the police came and asked me questions about what happened. It was the Fourth of July weekend. I lied and told them that we were in the yard with fireworks and a couple of guns and I accidentally got shot.

I was lying, but I was afraid if I sent them after this man, he was going to force them to kill him. I wanted him dead, but it was something I wanted to do myself. I have never in my life wanted to kill someone, but with him I did.

Why
I didn't leave
(until I did)

Why didn't I leave? Fear. Fear that he would kill me and himself if I would try to leave. Many times he said this to me. There were times I thought I could help him, and once in a while I could see a tiny bit of goodness in him. Those times were after he had beaten me. The next day he would become very sorry about what he had done, crying and telling me he wouldn't do it again. If it was real bad he would stop drinking and using drugs for a few days.

It was a very bad and dangerous relationship. At times I felt like I was his daughter because he would treat me like a child. Other times I was his sex toy that he would have his way with. Then at times I was an object that he hated and wanted to belittle; at those times I think he saw his mother in me. I was lost and full of fear about everything, and what made it so bad was I thought I had no one to turn to but him. Because he was so much older, I looked at him as a father figure, a lover, and a friend. It seems as if my heart was broken in all of these places and more.

After the shooting, things started to change once and for all. I only had hate in my heart for him.

I stayed in the hospital for a few hours, was treated, and called his father to come and pick me up. When we got home, Geechee Fred was nowhere to be found. I went out like a light, dreaming how I was going to kill this man.

That morning when I woke up, my mind started to drift into a dark place. I was feeling very strange and sad. I had to find a way in my mind not go into the deep depression I was heading for. I started calling people, seeking someone to talk to me and help pull me out of the hole. I called my twin sister, and she is the one who helped me from going deeper into that dark place. I told her what had happened. She actually wanted to get some of the family members to come up and kill Geechee Fred. I pleaded with her not to do that because I didn't want anyone to get in trouble. I said to her that I would be all right, that I would take care of it.

What brought me out of the depression was plotting ways to kill him. I knew that whatever I decided to do, whether with a knife or gun, I had to keep doing it until he wasn't moving. I can see why people who kill with a crime of passion become fearful that the person they are killing might get loose; that is how it becomes an overkill.

For days no one knew where he was. He was hiding in the woods, afraid I had told the police he had shot me. I went back to work to get myself involved with something to keep me from going back into that dark hole. My mind was taking me through all kinds of emotions.

Late one night about a week or so later, Geechee Fred showed up, looking like a madman, stinking and nasty. He was crying, begging, and pleading to me to please forgive him for what he had done. He said he was through with drinking and drugs and wanted me to help him to be a better man. Did I believe him? No!

I wanted to cut his throat for trying to fool me again. For a few weeks this man was clear, having no liquor or drugs. For about three weeks he did everything, trying to prove to me he was not lying; cleaning, cooking, and waiting on me hand and foot. I had never seen this side of him, but I knew this was just too good to be true—he looked like a phony and a coward. I stayed around so I could kill him and take some of the things that were left in the house that he didn't steal. His Dad had pretty much moved in with his girlfriend, so I wasn't that worried about him anymore.

My heart had hardened, and there was no way he could get back into my heart. Most of my life I've been able to tolerate a lot from people, but once I turned against you, there was no turning back. Slowly he started getting back to who he really was. First it was the liquor, one or two drinks—then the door was open and he went back to everything he'd been doing and more.

He started again with leaving home for days. When this started happening, I decided that I was ready to take him out. I had placed a couple of knives in the house that had very long blades on them, because when I hit him I wanted to hit the mark. I want to plunge the knife in and look into his eyes each time I hit him; I wanted to make it up-close and personal. I had a knife in my bedroom and one in the kitchen where I could quickly put my hands on one of them.

The day came when I was ready. He had been away from home all night. I was sitting on the porch when I saw him drive up in the car with the neighborhood crackhead princess. I was watching as he got out of the car, and for some reason the tiny woman got out of the car too. I didn't know her and didn't care about her. Both walked up on the porch and I didn't say one word.

Everything seemed to move in slow motion. I got up, went into the kitchen, and got the knife. I went back on the porch where they were, grabbed Geechee Fred by the throat, and pinned him against the wall. I raised my hand to strike him, but something happened to my arm. I couldn't move it. Something that was stronger than me held my arm. I looked up and it was this little tiny crackhead woman that held my arm. Where the strength came from out of this little woman at the time I did not know. I was twice her size if not more; I just could not move my arm.

Later on in life, and when I came to greater understanding of who I am, I knew it was God personally taking over of my life. I still had my hand on Geechee Fred's throat. I looked into his eyes, and all I could see was fear. I let go of him and said, "You are not worth my life." I turned him loose. The tiny woman took the knife. I went into the house, got my purse, and walked out. I went to a neighbor's house down the street and asked her to call a cab to take me to the Greyhound bus station so I could take a bus back to Miami and my family. On my way to the bus station, I had the cab stop by the liquor store so I could pick up a fifth of liquor.

I do not remember much on that trip back to Miami. All I knew was, I had me a bottle and I was on my way out of hell. When the bus pulled up to the station in Miami, my twin was standing at the door, and she told me it looks bad now but it's going to be all right. I just broke down and cried like a baby, because that one thought touched me so deeply.

I moved back into my Mom's house. She welcomed me with open arms and she didn't throw my wrongs in my face. I had let Geechee Fred turn me against my family, yet they didn't give up on me. On one of our trips from New York to South Florida, we had come down to visit my family—I asked my Mom to forgive me, and she had. When my family met Geechee Fred they all saw how much he had brainedwashed me, because in front of them I would wait on him hand and foot.

I crawled back to my Mom's house and she treated me like a child is supposed to be treated, with love and kindness, and she helped me to heal. I was ashamed and feeling very sorry for myself and went deeper and deeper into drinking. This went on for a few months, until one morning I woke up and found myself parked on the side of the road with an empty bottle of liquor. I was drunk in the car with the windows down and my purse open with the money showing. I will never forget that morning—I can still feel the sun beaming down on my face, and hear the noise of people and the traffic as people were heading to work. I had hit rock bottom with all the drinking; I would drink it down fast and go out like a light. I used drinking to kill the pain and most of the time after one of my nights of drinking I would feel more pain because I was guilty of what I might have done to myself. It became a vicious cycle of drinking to kill the pain, and then more pain, and drinking to kill that. I didn't care too much for it but I liked how quickly it would make me forget.

Sometimes when I was drinking I would pretend I was someone else; I was able to do things I couldn't do when I was just me. How did I get the money to keep going? All those months, I just gave up—old habits die hard. And then I would feel guilty about that, too.

That was the morning when I decided I wasn't going to cry anymore. I promised God that I would never take another drink, and I haven't. My sister helped me get a job as a cook at the daycare where she was working. I started getting back into life— watching those kids so full of life was very rewarding and helped with my healing.

Singing has always been healing for me too, of course. There was one song I would sing all the time, "Rough Side of the Mountain." One phrase from that song saved my life: "I'm climbing up on the rough side of the mountain, trying my best to make it in."

Well, I made it in. I decided to go back to school, and I started attending Wilfred Academy to get my license as a cosmetologist. While attending school and working on getting myself together, I got a call from Geechee Fred telling me how bad things were going for him. He said he'd gone to jail, and somehow or another he had escaped and drove to where his mother lived. He had no money and wanted me to help him get back to New York. After hearing his story, I decided to take a trip to where he was and give him some money to help him get back to New York. I talked my sister into helping me with the drive to where he was; it was about 150 miles from Miami. When we got there, he was in bad shape; it seemed like he hadn't shaved or taken a shower in months.

Why did I do that? It was, to me, my way of closing the book on him. I gave him more than he needed to make the drive to New York. Before we left Miami, I added up how much it would cost him with gas, tolls, and food. I got a chance to meet his brother, who was a preacher in that little town with a big church and a large congregation. He didn't want Geechee Fred acting like a fool in this little town and bringing embarrassment on him and his family. He didn't like his brother and wanted him gone. He wouldn't give Geechee Fred money to get him out of town, saying that the church board was watching him.

I took him the money, and of course he tried once more to see if I would come back with him. I told him there was no way on God's earth I would come back to him and the thought of it made me sick. When I said that to Geechee Fred, he got this horrified look on his face and backed away from me. Apparently, that is when he really realized that he had lost me completely.

When we returned to Miami, my sister told me something that just confirmed everything. While we were visiting him, she went with him to the store to pick up some beer and food. She said on their way back from the store, he pulled off in the woods and tried to attack her. She said she was too ashamed to tell me at the time. Sometimes in life, when it's time for someone to move out of your life, things keep happening until you see it is time for this person to move on.

After the trip to see Geechee Fred, I felt that a great burden had been lifted off my shoulders.

And just when I thought everything was going to be all right, I got another call. When he got to Maryland, he didn't have enough money to pay the tolls, so he decided to run through the tollgate. The police stopped him and found out he had a warrant back in Gretna. That crack had damaged his head and I am sure that's why they call people who use that stuff "crackheads." I'm sure the money I gave him ended up being used on drugs and that was why he ran out of money. Lucky for him, they didn't find any drugs on him, but he was put in jail because of the warrant he had in Gretna, and he had to pay the toll.

I called the sheriff in Gretna. They knew who I was and had great respect for Geechee Fred's father, and that's the only reason they released the warrant.

While Geechee Fred was in Florida visiting with his mother before that, he had met with his nephew who had just gotten out of prison. Geechee Fred's brother didn't care much for his son because he was into a life of crime. I called him and told him what had happened with his uncle, that he was in jail up in Maryland. I convinced him to take the Greyhound, go to where he was, and help drive Geechee Fred to New York. I sent money to his nephew because he wasn't on drugs and I was sure he would get things done.

Geechee Fred's nephew stayed in New York with him for about four months, until he saw how bad his uncle really was and had to leave.

Once his nephew left, I never received any more information about Geechee Fred. Geechee Fred was back in New York and I was happy to be away from him. I felt like I had closed the door on this man once and for all, and I was ready to go on with my life.

Happy and rebuilding my life in Miami

I was doing great in school. I worked hard and earned my GED. This was the first time in my life I was happy about myself.

I was still practicing Islam and had started going to the temple. That's when I found out the respect the Muslim men have for the women. What Geechee Fred was teaching me about Islam was all wrong; he had his own thing going on, and I was his only member. If we had been going to the temple he would have been in big trouble. The Nation of Islam does not put up with that type of abuse. I learned a lot of good things from the teaching—some of the things I agreed with, some I did not. I do love the way the Nation of Islam helped many brothers who were on drugs and had given up on life, to turn their lives around. I started dressing with more respect for myself and covering my head.

One thing I didn't like: I could not continue going into clubs singing. Also, the teaching to me was of the separation of black and white people, not coming together. I wanted to be in a place where we all love one another. Islam was definitely part of my healing—I found more pride in myself and how to forgive my brothers and sisters.

I still had this deep desire in me to sing, though. That was the main reason I followed Geechee Fred down the wrong path—for the sake of music. So I decided not to be a part of Islam and got back more into the world, focusing on me and music.

After two years, I finished school. I took the state board test twice and passed the second time. I got my cosmetology license and went to work in Supercuts. Supercuts would hire students right out of school and they would train you in their way of doing hair. The training was about six weeks; after you finished the training, you would start working in the salon. We were paid minimum wage and we kept all of our tips. All you did in Supercuts was cut and wash hair; this was not a full salon. I did very well building up a big clientele. People would come in and ask for me; that's how good I was. I worked in North Miami Beach and then rose to become a manager of one of the stores.

Life was good. This went on for a while, just working and doing a little singing here and there. There were no men in my life. I just kept working and saving money, so I could one day open my own shop.

This was around the time my New York City date and old friend, Sweet John, came down to visit me in Miami. I had kept in touch with him because we had become such good friends. I had told him about school and how well things were going, and that I wanted to have my own shop one day. John was so proud of how I got my life together, and he gave me money so I could have my own shop. With that and some of what I had saved, I bought a duplex apartment—I rented out one side, and lived in the other side. Both were two-bedroom units, and I turned one of my bedrooms into my beauty shop. Everything you would find in a beauty shop I had—styling chairs, mirrors on the wall, and a shampoo sink. I left Supercuts, started my own thing, and was doing very well. I met some people who became lifelong friends—after 20 years or so we are still in touch with each other.

I was doing some singing around town, hooking up with a few bands. I had a copy of the 45 and tapes of the music Geechee Fred and I had recorded in New York. I wanted to find a studio where I could make copies and preserve the recordings. I had some very good music and I didn't want to lose it.

I don't remember how I was introduced to King Joseph's studio, but somehow I got the phone number and made an appointment. This was a powerful individual. Just talking to him on the phone mesmerized me—his voice was so deep, Barry White had nothing on him.

When I met him in person, his appearance blew me away. He was about six-feet-two, and I found out later that he had been a professional football player. When I got to the studio he was very talkative and explained everything he had to do to save the music for me. He told me that he was a piano player—when he started to play, I stood there with my mouth open in amazement at the sounds this man was making come out of that piano. I stayed with him for hours as he was talking, playing the piano, and showing me some of the things he had recorded at his studio. I fell in love with his talents and wanted to sit at his feet and learn.

He told me he taught vocal lessons at another studio in Fort Lauderdale and that he was starting to teach in his own studio too. I told him I wanted to take vocal lessons. He asked me to sing a song for him and I did one of Billie Holiday's songs. He said he loved my voice but did not like that Billie Holiday sound in my voice.

For some reason I always thought I had to have a man in charge of me, and once more I was about to let a man take control of my life.

King Joseph

I started going to King Joseph's studio for vocal lessons and working on saving my music. I called King Joseph a king because to me he had all the qualities of a great African king. He was a child prodigy, playing music at age four. Not only was he a genius on the piano, he was a master on the saxophone and he played other instruments as well. He was a genius with his music and in the studio. I just wanted to be around him all the time.

Soon I found out he had a lady friend named Eve. She was madly in love with King Joseph and very jealous. In the beginning I didn't see the jealousy, but every time I went to the studio Eve would show up. She didn't have a car, so she would come with him or catch the bus.

Eve and I became very close. She wanted to be my friend and she was a lonely woman. King Joseph worked all the time and they never did things together. I found out later what was going on with him. When I would give her rides home or we went out someplace, her conversation was constantly about him. One thing I learned in life, you do not keep telling another woman about your man.

I really enjoyed her company. King Joseph was never around the house when I went to pick her up to take her shopping or go out. The only time I would see him is when I went to the studio for my lessons; I would do the lesson and get out of there. I have always had rules when it came to another woman's man—if you are my friend, I will not mess with your man, and by then a married man was off my list too. When I went to the studio, King Joseph would make advances at me but I ignored them. I kept going to the studio because of everything I was learning from him about music.

After months of Eve and I being friends, one day she just cut me loose. She stopped coming to the studio. I would call and she wouldn't pick up the phone. She became very angry at me; and would not tell me why. There were times I went to her house, and she wouldn't open the door. I asked King Joseph what was going on. He said he didn't know, but their relationship was falling apart.

I kept going to the studio and Eve never reached out to me, she stayed away. I felt that King Joseph was beginning to really like me. Each and every time I went to the studio he was after me. One day I decided to have sex with him, and we agreed to have one night of sex and then we would never see each other again.

He got a hotel room on Miami Beach; it was truly beautiful. I met him at the hotel and we had a hot night of passionate lovemaking. I just let myself go because I knew that after this night I would not see him again. When morning came, I kissed him and said goodbye. I never called him after that night. He would call me but I wouldn't take the calls; I even changed my phone number. I stopped going to the studio and started working on how to forget him. He didn't know where I lived—I'm sure if he did, he would have shown up at my door.

I had completely stopped going to the studio and put the music on hold for a while. I didn't go out to any of the clubs any more, I just got busy working on building my hair business. Working hard kept my mind off of the man and the music.

In life, most of the time when you are running from something, one day it will catch you. It had been more than a year since I had seen him and I will never forget the day he showed back up in my life; it was a shock to my system. I had gone shopping in the North Miami area which was about ten miles from where I was living. I was in a thrift store, looking for some things I could put in my hair salon.

When I felt the powerful energy all around me, I knew it was him. He came behind me, and I was afraid to turn around. King Joseph was huge and solid as a rock, and I could feel all this chemistry coming from him. I tried to get away from him, but his days of playing football came back. He blocked me like he was a solid wall. I couldn't get away, he wouldn't let me get away, but did I really want to get away?

He wanted to know why I ran away from him. I said I didn't want to cause any further problems between him and Eve, I just wanted to get out of the picture. That is when he told me that they had broken up, that he loved me, wanted me to be with me. Once again I put my trust in a man and believed everything this man said to me. We all get those warnings when something isn't right and most of the time I would ignore them and pay the price.

King Joseph was a great vocal teacher and he taught me how to give vocal lessons. I became very good at it and started having my own students. Around this time he gave me a key to the studio. I became so involved with him and the music that I started slipping away from my hair business; people would make appointments with me and I would forget.

The studio was in a two-story warehouse. His office was upstairs, and downstairs is where he had the studio control room, and another big room where he taught vocal lessons and had talent shows. We used to put on little shows for the students to learn about being in front of an audience. This is where I learned more about recording and working in a studio—he would write songs for me and record them. I was in love with this man and crazy about the way he made me feel, and the music made it so wonderful. I would stay there for days with him, working on music and making love.

Once he was in the studio, he would work for hours recording and editing music, and I would be at his feet just

wanting to please him in any way he wanted. Once again I became a fool for a man, trusting in everything he said and did.

I still did not get it that in life God must be first. Put no one or anything before God or yourself. I still wasn't being responsible for myself. Most of the time I was with him, he didn't have a car; I would let him use mine. He would take my car and would disappear for days. I was all right with that because I knew he was coming back to me. It wasn't that bad because the store wasn't that far away and I could catch the bus. This went on for a while. I had forgotten about my shop and spent most of my time at the studio.

When he wasn't there, I would work on my music. He made all kinds of tracks for me to sing with. Sometimes, when I wasn't working with him at some of our club dates, I would go out and do some one-hour shows with the tracks he made.

When he would leave the studio, I didn't know where he went, and I didn't ask.

One day I had caught the bus to go to my house, when I saw my car parked at an apartment building that wasn't far from the studio. For weeks I didn't tell him I saw the car, but then something happened and I had to go looking for him. I was at the studio when the lights went off—he had forgotten to pay the electric bill. To make things worse, we had appointments that evening for him to do some recording. I started calling everywhere trying to reach him, and then my mind flashed back to where I had seen my car at that apartment.

It was about a mile and a half from the studio and I decided to walk there. I knocked on the door of the apartment where the car was parked. I heard his voice asking who is it and slowly he came to the door. When he opened the door, I heard a woman in the background asking who it was, and it was Eve's voice. I told him the lights were off and reminded him of his later appointments.

I went back to the studio to wait. I didn't know what to think or what was going on with him and Eve.

When he came back to the studio, he played with my head big-time. King Joseph had been in Vietnam, and I'd been told never to piss him off, because you didn't want to see the violent side of him. When he did come back, the lights were still off. He came in, went to the control room, had a seat, and pulled out a gun. He said he was tired of not having the money to do the things he wanted to do and that he was ready to give up on life. He said he would kill himself but that first he would blow me away because he did not want to leave me.

I started crying and begging him not to do that. He was holding the gun in his lap, and I sat across his lap. With the gun under me, I put my arm around his neck, kissed and hugged him, telling him that everything was going to be all right and to put the gun away.

Looking back on that, I really was a fool. The man shocks the hell out of me so I wouldn't bring up him and Eve. He put the gun away and in a few minutes the lights came on. I never did bring up anything about him and Eve. King Joseph was so damn good that she and I would work together sometimes in the studio after that, and had no problem with each other. She had the man when he went home, and I had him when he was at the studio.

There were more women, too—I would go in search of things and found them. I found a video of him making out with one of the ladies who came to the studio to do some recording, and I found out he had two boys from another lady. There were times he would bring the children to the studio, and sometimes their mother.

He never explained anything to me or to Eve either—we just accepted it. He was a very silent man who very rarely raised his voice; he just did what he did and you took it.

I was a damn fool. I was so proud to be the one to be near him the most. He placed me by his side in the studio where he spent most of his time. While I was with him, I wrote a few songs, and some we wrote together. One song I wrote was about his women and me—the name of the song is "Hey Girlfriend." The song went something like this:

Hey, girlfriend, there's something I got to tell you,
The man you're loving I'm loving him too,
The way he makes you feel too mean that's nothing new,
He's thinking about me while making love to you.

King Joseph and I started singing in supper clubs around town as a duo; I was the singer, and he was on keyboards and singing with me.

We had a good thing going on, singing in some of the best clubs in South Florida. I would dress in beautiful gowns, and he wore his suits, sometimes a tux. This was a very good time in my life because I was doing what I love, singing. I paid a big price being with this man but I didn't mind because he was teaching me so many things about music.

When I first got with King Joseph, I was still afraid of going onstage and singing in front of people. He helped me overcome that. One thing he did was to train me in how to present myself onstage; this is what he taught me, and I taught it to the vocal students.

Music is one of the reasons I followed that fool Geechee Fred out of town and down the wrong road. It took me a lot of years and pain to find out it was all about the music. All I went through from Mississippi as a child, from my birth to 60 years later, was about music. It took me all those years to find out why God put me here; and King Joseph was just one more of my teachers along the way.

Things were going well with King Joseph and me—going out on our club dates, working on recordings at the studio, and the great sex. We had a regular club date in a supper club called Top of The Home. It was on top of a bank building in what you might call the penthouse. It was made in a circle with glass all around, and you could look out and see the whole city.

When people came into the club and said they wanted to hear me sing, I would downplay myself so they would listen to him. I remember one night a customer asked me to sing "Good Morning Heartache" and gave me $200 for singing it. Most of my life, people would always tell me I have a beautiful voice, but I didn't get it; I just couldn't hear what people were hearing.

One night King Joseph was onstage doing a few numbers before it was time for me to go on, when some man came up and wanted to sit with me. I told him no. I turned and looked up to the stage, and King Joseph give me a very strange look—something that looked like hate. This was around the time I started seeing changes in his moods. The more we get involved with what I call outsiders, the weirder he would act. He had his own world going on and didn't want anyone disturbing it. I just let that one pass and forgot about it.

It was a long time before I saw that look again, because I wouldn't talk with any other men. The owner moved to a new location and wanted us to go with him to the new club; he booked us for five days a week. In this club, he had two rooms—one side was the supper club where we played, and the other side was the dance club. We would start playing around 6:00 p.m. and stop at 10:00, and in the next room across the hall the dance band would kick off around 11:00 and go until 4:00 in the morning.

We had been working at the club for about six months when something went down that turned my heart against King Joseph. I was sitting at a table waiting for my time to go onstage. King Joseph was up there doing what he did so well, playing his heart out. Some white man asked me to dance with him—I guess I had forgotten what had happened before when King Joseph acted so strange.

This man wouldn't take no for an answer, so I danced with him. Then I saw that King Joseph had this vicious look on his face—so I just stopped dancing and went back to my table. For the rest of the night he didn't say anything to me, and I had this funny feeling that something bad was going to happen.

Once the show was over for the night, we packed up our things to head for home. On our job he would drive my car, take me home, and pick me up the next day for work. We were driving south on the turnpike heading back to Miami when he looked at me and very quietly said, "I'm going to kill you because you let that man touch you." I told him I was sorry, that it didn't mean a thing, it was just a drunk that I had to brush off. He was very angry, but it didn't show in his voice or face, it was the way he was talking. He said he was going to cut me up and take my body out to Alligator Alley and feed me to the alligators.

That is when I became full of fear of this man. As we were driving down the road at 75 miles an hour, he turned the wheel loose and started beating my face and head with his fists. I started begging and pleading with him to please just take me home. When he had finished, he put his hands back on the wheel and took me home. Why the car didn't go off the road I do not know.

When I got home, my head hurt all over. I looked in the mirror, and one of my eyeballs looked like it was hanging out. I had to go to the emergency room because I didn't want to lose my eye. They did save it, and I had to wear a patch over that eye.

Later on that day, I got a call from King Joseph telling me to be ready for work that evening. I told him I had to go to the hospital, but he said he didn't give a damn, just be ready for work. He came that evening to pick me up and showed no remorse, just like nothing had happened.

When it was time for me to go onstage with that patch on my eye, I was full of shame. When it came time for me to sing, he played the intro to the song, and I couldn't get any sound to come out of my throat because of the big lump there. My heart was in so much pain that I couldn't bring the words out. He played the intro twice, and I just stood there, when he shouted at me to sing. What came was tears. With the pain I was feeling and him screaming at me, I did start to sing, and I put all those feelings into that song—and got a standing ovation.

Despite my fear of him, we kept working. What made things better was when he put in other people to play with us, a guitar player and a drummer. This did take off some of the tension. But I thought about wanting him to die. I knew he had some type of heart problem, something that ran in his family.

For about two years we worked in the club, and then the owner said he had to close down because of health reasons. We were back working in the studio and teaching vocal lessons.

One day he asked if I would like to go out on the road with a friend of his, a comedian. Wildman Steve was his name—he would come to the studio from time to time for King Joseph to make tapes for him to sell on his shows. Wildman traveled throughout the South putting on his X-rated show, and he was very good at it. King Joseph said that the experience would be good for me. I was afraid and didn't want to go. I was still having panic attacks and didn't want to leave my comfort zone, and King Joseph was my safe person. No matter what I said, King Joseph didn't go for it; he pushed me out the door. He made four tapes; each one had eight songs, and each tape was a show for me to open for Wildman. Yes, I did go out on the road. I learned a lot, too—Wildman was a very good businessman. He booked all the shows and handled all the money. I am sure he cut me short a few times, but all and all I had a good time.

Eventually, King Joseph told me that a well-known singer wanted him to be the leader of his band and go out on the road with him. He said things were not going well at the studio. The rent had gone up, and he just couldn't afford it any more. I knew things weren't going well, and the way I felt about him had changed, too. He decided to close it down. I helped him pack up and moved everything to storage with him.

Sheba and Wildman Steve

We said our goodbyes. From time to time he would come back into town, every three or four months to check on his storage, and we would see each other for a little fun. I did not like the man, but loved the sex and music.

One day I didn't see him anymore. The last thing I heard was that he had passed away and today I'm still not sure about that.

While working at the studio during those many times he would leave and be gone for days, I made all kinds of tracks— some of them I still have today.

I took the tracks with me and started working around town doing a solo act.

Sheba and the Rhythm Kings

I was doing very well around town, singing at different clubs' happy hours. I got real popular with my music. At one particular club call Rand's, most of the people who came in had good jobs. They would stop in after work for drinks before going home. Some of them had lovers on the side, and would have a quickie before going home. There was a lot of sex going on. At this time I was in charge of my life. I didn't have a man in my life at that time but I still had the feeling that I had to have a man.

Before breaking up with King Joseph, a guitar player named Rob Moore told King Joseph that he was looking for a singer for his blues band. King Joseph told Rob I would be perfect for that. This opened up a whole new world for me, singing with a live band, singing the music that I was born to sing. When we started going out on the road, Rob had quite a few gigs lined up in the Florida Keys. We worked a few jobs in the Fort Lauderdale area too.

One of the main places we played was a club called the Poor House. It was a blues club with the look of one of those old joints. We would start at 10:00 and play until 2:00. The house was always packed. This is around the time I found out that not only was I a singer, I was an entertainer because I knew how to work the crowd—I would make the people get up and dance and just have fun.

There was some talk about the Riverwalk Blues Festival. The Poor House was one of the sponsors, and they wanted me to be one of singers on that stage.

I was still working my single jobs and some parties when I wasn't working with the band. One night I was doing my happy hour show at a club called Randy's Miami. Two men walked into the club—one was white, the other one was black—and they sat at the bar. You couldn't help but notice them, as they were both more than six feet tall and damn good-looking. They ordered a drink and were watching me, nodding and smiling at each other.

When I stopped to take a break, they said they wanted to talk to me. The white guy's name was Ken Minahan, but his nickname was Snowman because his long hair was almost as white as his skin. He was a guitar player. Reed Roberts, the other man, said he was a bass player. They told me they were looking to form a band—they had heard about me and wanted me to be a part of the band. They said they had a bad ass drummer by the name of Rocking John, and when I met him, they were right. This man had a powerful hand—he played those drums like chopping wood, and he would always keep his eye on the singer; that is the sign of a great drummer. They wanted me to be the lead singer. Both Snowman and Reed were great backup singers—it was amazing the high notes Reed could hit. Reed was from Georgia and was a part of the Roach Thompson Blues Band—they were a blues big band, complete with horns, and were well known all over Florida, Georgia, and Alabama. Snowman was from Chicago, and all his life he'd loved the blues.

I agreed to join the band, and somehow or another the Poor House-sponsored concert at the Riverwalk Blues Festival happened with our new band, which we named Sheba and the Rhythm Kings.

Snowman was very good at promoting the band. We worked all over the Florida Keys and other places. In Key Largo at the Ocean Reef Club, we started the blues club called Harbor House of Blues, and the members were so kind with their tips that we were able to produce our first CD called "Ms. Good-n-Plenty." That CD is my life story in the blues. Each song was a story about a stepping stone of what went on in my life. These were good times. I was even interviewed in a U.K. publication, *ROCKnREEL* (*RnR* for short). I've redone the CD through Bongo Boy Record Company; it's called "Sheba the Mississippi Queen: A Real Good Woman" (see p. 127).

Being an unsigned group, we played quite a few major concerts. Snowman booked jobs all the way from Florida to Alabama, Georgia, Mississippi, and Memphis.

Once, when we were booked near Jackson, Mississippi, on the night of our show a woman from the local radio station came in. She told me about an incident that had just happened. A black boy had been going out with a white man's daughter, and one morning they found the boy hanging in a tree with all the life out of him. It was said he killed himself because the father had told the daughter she couldn't see him anymore, but nobody believed that. All the black leaders locally and nationally, even Rev. Jackson and Al Sharpton, were working to find out what actually went down.

I told her about Billie Holiday's travels in the deep South and a song that had been written for her. She traveled with an all-white

Sheba and the Rhythm Kings

band, but she saw all kinds of things that were happening to black people, and it was very disturbing to her. In the late 1930s, a New Yorker named Abel Meeropol saw a photograph of a lynching and wrote a song, "Strange Fruit," about it. After he played it for the owner of a club in New York, the club owner passed it along to Billie Holiday. The "strange fruit" refers to the black bodies swaying from the trees. I was invited to sing the song on the radio station.

While I was with the Rhythm Kings, I was getting pretty lonely. I met another fool who was a pure alcoholic. At the time I didn't realize alcohol could do a person so bad. There were warning signs but I ignored them. I married the man—and four months later, I started working on getting a divorce. I called him Wizened Eye Kim. At the time I was so into the church that I didn't want to have sex and not be married; I was still practicing Islam in my own way and I went stupid for a moment.

I sang with the Rhythm Kings for about four or five years before things come to an end. I was almost 50 years old when the band ended, and once again I went back to my tracks for a little while. Snowman went to Thailand and formed a band over there. He invited me to come over and join the band, but I was still thinking about security and having a man in my life.

Sheba and B.B. King

118

Cycles of life

My life has had many ups and downs—that is the way life is supposed to be. After growing up, I realized they were all stepping stones to get me to where I am today. I have the understanding of who I am, and who God is. I can forgive, and have forgiven, each and every person who ever did anything to me. I have asked, if there's anyone I have wronged, to forgive me, whether they are dead or alive. I do not need to hear from you to see whether or not you accept my forgiveness. I know when the word is spoken and is out in the universe, it is done, and so it is.

I have become a part of New Thought, and have learned a lot about forgiveness and that I was responsible for myself and all the stuff I drew into my life. When you do not forgive and hold on to grudges, this can kill you. This has been a hard lesson for me to learn. I think not forgiving has caused most of the sickness in my life because I wouldn't let things go that had happened to me. I found comfort in food and became very overweight. I developed diabetes, high blood pressure, had to have a pacemaker, and endured total knee replacements on both knees.

For so long I kept looking for my help "out there" in people and things. When I found out all the help that I needed was inside of me, that was hard to believe. After all the unkind things I had done to myself and let others do to me, it was hard. I can no longer blame anyone with what was going on with me. Coming up in the Baptist Church, you blame the devil; in Unity, you are totally responsible for yourself; there is no devil.

My whole life I have been searching and searching for this something—now I can say I have found that something. It is now time for me to keep on growing spiritually, because I have connected with The Christ that is within me, that part of God that is part of me. I always thought that my help came from somewhere out there. In order for me be whole, I had to find something out there to help me to be better and feel better. I did all of that; I turned myself over easily to other people so they could help me live my life, or for them to live it for me. That is not a good thing to do; most of the time, people have a hard time just trying to live their own life, they do not need a monkey on their back. So when they do all kinds of vicious things, you shouldn't get mad because you gave them your power; never let anyone possess or process your spirit.

In the beginning of my spiritual journey, it was very hard for me to accept that all the stuff I went through, truthfully, I brought on myself. I wanted to blame the people who did those things to me; I wanted them to hurt because they hurt me. I looked for all kinds of things to help me, especially a man. For more than 60 years I have been running away from me—at least I gave it a good try. When I did not find my happiness in those things, I had a love affair with food, and in the end it disappointed me. I became what they called obese—when I first heard that word coming from the doctor, it sound like some kind of animal; I said, that can't be me.

Yes, I feel like I have lived many lifetimes in this one lifetime. It seemed my life would do a flip every ten years. The first ten years was from my birth and Mississippi. The next ten years was Florida. The next ten years were in New York with that fool Geechee Fred, though I was with him a little more than fifteen years. The next few years was coming back to Florida, going to school, hooking up with King Joseph. The next ten years was the time I spent with my band the Rhythm Kings, working all over, and recording my first CD.

As I was getting older, the time for the big flips started getting shorter. I married a man, Clarence, and to this day I do believe he was my soulmate. He was a wonderful man—he was the only person who knew what type of person I was. He didn't judge me with looks, it was about feeling with him. He was blind. He had glaucoma and started going blind in his 50s—he knew it was going to happen, and he prepared himself for it. Through him, he made my dream come true of wanting to have a child. We adopted a beautiful little girl.

He was much older, and people sometimes would assume I was his daughter. He was such a gentleman—he was very kind and gentle with me, and he helped me to heal. I met him in my

50s—he was in his 80s and already was totally blind. He was the one to encourage me to do more about my education, and I started attending college in my 50s. He believed in me more than I believed in myself at the time. He loved my voice, and sometimes I would sing to him all those old songs from back in his time. My husband was the one who encouraged me to record my CD "Butter on My Rolls" and he paid for the whole thing. My husband was a part of Christian Science; we were on the same spiritual journey. I started getting deeper into my spiritual studies. Together, we attended Universal Truth Center in Miami.

My husband passed away—he didn't last the ten years—but he did leave me a wonderful gift, my daughter. While my husband was alive, I wanted to tell him some of what went on in my past, and he said to me, "It isn't what you did in the past, it's what you are doing now."

On our third anniversary, he gave me another gift: he presented me with a plaque in the shape of a heart that I will treasure forever; he called me his angel. The men in my life had called me many things, but never an angel, although I'd given them my all.

ANGEL
March 19, 2005

Angel, three years ago, I was lonely, searching for someone to fill my void. Angel Sheba appeared to me in a dental office. I had no way to know that she was the one sent to me by the divine director, but now I'm certain that you were God sent. Little did I know that you would be the person that I would spend the rest of my life with. On this our wedding day I thank God for you and may our love last forever.

Love always,
Clarence

After my husband's passing, I moved out of the city because there was so much crime. I wanted to find a safer place to raise our child. I continued going to school and working on my spiritual journey by going to Unity, taking classes, and reading all kinds of books on spirituality. I feel my life is on a new track, a spiritual journey—I made it to the mountaintop and now it is time to enjoy the fresh air. On my journey in this lifetime, I made many mistakes; some call it "missing the mark." The greatest one I might have made was that God gave me a gift for singing, and in the beginning I wasn't passionate enough with it. I didn't take control of my God-given gift. I let others tell me how to handle it, or let them tell me to shut up and leave it alone.

One thing I have to say to others about the gifts you brought to the world, is to express them—do not let anything or anyone stand in your way. If it is from God, it is a good thing, and when you don't use them, or when you let others take them away from you, that's when you go wrong.

My Mom and Clarence

My spirituality and my music today

When I was child, every Sunday we had to go to church and be in Sunday school. When I became a teenager, I got away from church and was living on the wild side of life. I was doing everything I was big enough to do.

At one point I got scared and went back into the church trying to find the God of my youth. When I did get back into the church, I still didn't find what I was looking for—it was all talk about a God who created me in sin and was out to get me. I went to all kinds of churches but didn't find the truth. People were saying one thing and doing another. In my young adult years, I stayed full of fear and was constantly looking for someone else to help me.

I got turned off from those churches because what they were teaching didn't seem true. I just couldn't understand a God that would give to one and not to another, a God that is watching all the things you say or do, and if you did anything wrong He will punish you. This was a Santa Claus God "who knows when you are sleeping and knows when you're awake, so you'd better be good for goodness sake."

What I enjoyed the most with some of the churches was the music. There were wonderful gospel groups that used to go from church to church singing old-fashioned gospel music, and I really enjoyed that. There were even times I would get up and sing too. The only thing about that was, I couldn't sing in church and then go out and sing in clubs; it was a conflict to me at the time.

Still in search of myself and what life was all about, I started studying a lot of New Age books; I was seeing things that I could relate to. I think the first books I started studying were by Marianne Williamson, Caroline Myss, Dr. Wayne Dyer, and Deepak Chopra, to name a few. Most of these books helped me begin to get deeper into meditation and look for my answers from within myself.

The first Unity church I went to was in Miami under the leadership of Rev. Dr. Johnnie Colemon. She was a student of the founders of Unity, Charles and Myrtle Fillmore. In the '50s, she went to Unity Village to study. At first, she wasn't allowed to stay on campus because she was black, but in 1955, she became the first African-American to live at Unity Village, in a cottage set apart. She became an ordained Unity minister in 1957. She was the founder of Christ Unity Center in the '50s, and in 1974 she established her own denomination, the Universal Foundation for Better Living, and led the Christ Universal Temple in Chicago. I give thanks to this great woman who went through so much shame to bring this teaching to the black community.

I kept coming back to Unity because I felt in my heart it was the right place to be and what I'd been longing for most of my life. I found out that God is a loving God and that God was not out to get me. God does not punish us for our sins, we punish ourselves. The God she was speaking of was not way up in the sky somewhere—that God is within me.

I started to look at people differently because the same God that is in me is in everybody. I learned one of the major laws of life is to forgive, because not forgiving causes all kinds of problems in your body and mind—high blood pressure, heart attacks, diabetes, and many more problems.

I have within me an inner guidance that I trust to guide my life. I have a powerhouse within me that is The Christ. I no longer look to man for my answers, I go to The Christ first.

Now that I know that The Christ is within me, I am guided by it and it has been the biggest growth of my life. I sing now because this is my gift to the world, and God speaks through my voice. Whether it's blues, jazz, gospel—it is all God. Whoever I can touch with this gift from God, I want to do it and do it to the best of my ability. It is a gift not for me, but to share with the world. Being guided by God, I produced a CD called "Blues in The Keys of Inspiration." On that CD, I sing about a loving God who is within us.

Still, if I were to meet Jesus now, I would ask him, "Brother, would you please tell me, what is this all about? Why do we exist?" Most of all I would ask, "How I can be like you? You did leave us the Bible with instructions, but men have tried to change so much of what you were saying because they want to be in control."

I've been asked what I would tell my younger self if I could go back and do so.

To my 12-year-old self, I would say, don't let anyone possess your spirit. There are a lot of things your Mom doesn't know but she loves you and wants the best for you. Don't let anyone bully you and run you off from school. Stay in school and get your education so you can be all you can be. You are a beautiful girl. You are very smart and you have a lot to offer to the world; but you must let it grow within you.

To my 25-year-old self, I would say, you have a wonderful gift within you that is your voice. Don't let anyone take control of this—you can take control of your own gift. Don't let anyone push you around. Stand up for yourself, fight back. When they throw a blow, throw a blow back. Keep punching back—soon you will see the fear in the other person and they will leave you alone. You must be willing to die for you so you can live.

Some things I would say to a young girl or a young woman—one of the most important things in life is to know yourself. Don't look for anyone else to tell you who you are, find out for yourself. One of the first things to do is to find that inner strength that is within you. Let God be your guide. You must educate yourself in all things so you can have a better life. You were created to do a particular thing on earth that really nobody else can do. Find out what that is.

You are precious and a gift from God.

When you are ready for someone special in your life, let that person be just as precious as you are.

If you are following your inner guidance, there will be signs along the way showing you. Don't ignore the signs.

I'm in my 60s now, and my passion and activity in music have just continued to grow.

I guess now is as good a time as any to tell you about my name. Many years ago, I changed my name from Martha because I felt that it was a slave name. I picked the name Sheba Makeda because of Queen Makeda, who was a queen of an ancient country called Sheba. That territory is now known as Ethiopia in Africa and Yemen in the Middle East. From what I read in the Bible and some history books, she is the same queen who went to visit King Solomon. During the slave trade, there were many kings and queens transported to North America. This lineage and knowledge were taken from us, but no one can take away the way you feel inside. Who's to say I'm not a queen? I also learned to embrace my Mississippi history. And so, I am Sheba the Mississippi Queen.

My newest CD, "A Real Good Woman," was released by Bongo Boy Records at the same time as this book. Every song on my CD tells a story of something going right or wrong in my life. Just as when I was a kid, I knew that if I put music to it, it would keep me away from drinking, drugs, and the doctor.

"Dance Jump" is what I call a happy blues. Lots of people think that all blues are sad. This song is when you've been working all week and just want to blow off some steam.

"A Real Good Woman" is the song of my heart. All my life, I've been looking for a real good man. Every man I've been with has played me for a fool, cheated on me, or beat the hell out of me, except for my last husband—Clarence showed me kindness, gentleness, and what true love really is, and helped me to heal.

"Big Man" is about a man who has a big heart and knows how to love, and not only sexually. On the other hand, some people might think that old-fashioned way—you know what they say about black men, and that works too.

"Can't Help Loving My Man"—if you have ever been in love, this song is it. The man I was in love with at the time (King Joseph) helped me write it. I was a fool in love. Then I found out that I wasn't the only one in love with him, he had three others and the kids to go along with it. I left with my heart ripped out and he tried to rip my eyeball out.

"Oh So Good" is another one of those happy blues songs, just so happy with the way my man made me feel at the moment.

"Pouring Rain" is a song that someone wrote for me. At the time I felt like I was standing alone in the rain, crying.

"Blues of My Soul" is all about my Mom getting us out of Mississippi. It's kind of hard for me to believe that we lived like that.

"Butter on My Roll" is another song that someone wrote for me. I just love the feeling of that song.

"Tell Me Why"—I was asking all the people in my life, and not only the men, but everyone—why do you treat me so badly? What did I do to you for you to treat me so bad?

"Don't Say Goodbye" is a song I wrote when I was around 25 years old. I was filled with fear and dependent on that man who was beating on me and had me traveling down a bad road. I was saying goodbye to all my family and friends because he had taken me a long way from home. For eight years, my family didn't even know where I was.

"Hey Girlfriend" is a song I wrote because I was mad at my man and the women he had. I was telling them that I was his biggest fool and wanted to keep it that way.

"Ms. Good-n-Plenty" is a song I wrote for all the big ladies saying that we are very passionate and know how to pleasure our man, because we put a lot into it. In our heads we feel the same as anyone else. We are the same, just more of us to love, and if you don't know how to love a big lady we will show you how.

"Good Good Loving" really drives it home. It tells you what we want, how we want it, and where we want it. This is why I love the blues—you can really put your heart and soul into it. The blues can be happy, sad, or full of sex. It's how you feel, but most of all you must live it. The blues picked me because it knew we would be good for each other.

Life is what makes a good blues singer. Blues is about life and the things that life takes you through. It's about bad times, good times, loving someone and not being loved back. That's why people don't accept a young person singing the blues—they feel they haven't really lived it. Someone said, "The blues is easy to play but hard to feel." The blues would be best described as stories, about people highlighting their feelings in music, the good and bad.

The blues is our trail of tears, blood, and sweat coming from the dry bones of those who died for us. So many lost their lives so we could be free and we're not standing up for them. There are too many of us who do not care about our music, the blues.

For the African-American, the blues is like a history book that we need to study and learn from. Our brothers and sisters, the white people, I thank them for carrying on the blues and taking it places that we as black people couldn't take it. It needs to be known to our black children that the blues is America's first homegrown music. We must teach it to our children and carry on this great tradition.

Keb Mo and Sheba

Sheba with some of her family. Donald, Sheba, Mary, Joseph

Sheba's late brother-in-law, Larry Marshall, creator of the first Reggae record, "Nanny Goat"

Sheba with Nikki Hill

*Sheba with
Shemekia Copeland*

Sheba with her twin sister, Mary

www.ingramcontent.com/pod-product-compliance
Lightning Source LLC
Chambersburg PA
CBHW071820090426
42737CB00012B/2145